"Simon Kim expands the story of the Catholic Church in the United States beyond the more familiar narratives of European and Latin . American immigration to show the unique gifts that Asian Catholics bring. More than just history or sociology, Kim narrates the confluence of Vatican II, immigration reform, and the civil rights movement in the 1960s as movements of the Holy Spirit, the fruits of which we are just beginning to appreciate today. This book is a timely and beautiful contribution to unity through diversity in the US Catholic Church."

—William T. Cavanaugh
    Director of Center for World Catholicism and Intercultural
        Theology (CWCIT)
    Professor of Catholic Studies at DePaul University

"This book is a careful reflection of the courageous theological journey from Vatican II to its impact on Asian immigrant communities in North America. It is truly a development to be celebrated."

—Wonsuk Ma
    Oxford Centre for Mission Studies
    Executive Director, David Yonggi Cho Research Tutor
        of Global Christianity

"As he did in his previous book *Memory and Honor*, in *A World Church in Our Backyard*, Simon C. Kim has given us a book that we really needed! Kim begins to fill in the problematic gaps in our theological and cultural understanding of contemporary immigration and cultural diversity in the United States, especially in reference to the smaller but more rapidly growing migrations from East Asia and the Pacific. For Kim, Vatican II is a critical transition point not only in the Church's approach to the world (as often assumed and here explored in theological depth) but also in the US Church's approach to immigration and immigrants. He invites us to examine both of these re-orientations not just as watershed moments for Church leadership but as changes in Catholic ecclesiology itself."

—Brett C. Hoover
    Assistant Professor of Theological Studies
    Loyola Marymount University

A World Church in Our Backyard

How the Spirit Moved
Church and Society

Simon C. Kim

A Michael Glazier Book

LITURGICAL PRESS
Collegeville, Minnesota

www.litpress.org

A Michael Glazier Book published by Liturgical Press

Cover design by Monica Bokinskie. Collage by Alyssa Storm.

1   2   3   4   5   6   7   8   9

Library of Congress Cataloging-in-Publication Data

Names: Kim, Simon C., author.
Title: A world church in our backyard : how the spirit moved church and society / Simon C. Kim.
Description: Collegeville, Minnesota : Liturgical Press, 2016. | "A Michael Glazier book." | Includes bibliographical references.
Identifiers: LCCN 2015047637 (print) | LCCN 2015048651 (ebook) | ISBN 9780814687611 (pbk.) | ISBN 9780814687772 (ebook)
Subjects: LCSH: Catholic Church—History—1965– | Vatican Council (2nd : 1962–1965 : Basilica di San Pietro in Vaticano)
Classification: LCC BX1390 .K54 2016 (print) | LCC BX1390 (ebook) | DDC282/.73089—dc23
LC record available at http://lccn.loc.gov/2015047637

To William "Padre Bill" Barman
For our friendship and ministry in serving a world church

Contents

Foreword

If there is a master narrative of the Catholic Church in the United States, it is one built on the experience of immigration. Although this theme does not account for the presence of Catholics in the South and Southwest who became part of the US Church when the border between the United States and Mexico "moved" in the nineteenth century, it has come to prevail, both in Catholic and Protestant accounts of the history of the Church in this country. That story has been told from the perspective of European immigration, from the formation of the colony of Maryland in the eighteenth century, down through the migrations from southern and eastern Europe in the early twentieth century.

After the closing of the doors of entry to the United States with the Immigration Act of 1924, some historians felt that the immigration phase of the US Church was now largely completed. For many, the Hart-Celler Act of 1965, which reopened those doors—and opened them more widely to immigrants from Asia for the first time—continued that older immigration narrative. But there were significant differences. This time, the major flow was not from Europe but from Latin America, the Caribbean, and Asia. Fifty years on, we are still very much in the midst of this new era. And the full implications are now just beginning to appear.

The majority of attention thus far has been given to the Latin American immigration, since it is without doubt the numerically largest one. Its contours are already clear: over 50 percent of all US Catholics under the age of thirty-five have this Latin American heritage. What this means for the coming two decades is only now coming up for serious discussion. What is already apparent is that the current immigration cannot be read solely through the lens of previous immigrations from Europe. Rather, it must be seen through lenses crafted by the distinctive experiences of the immigrant groups now entering the country, the current situation of the United States, and the impact of a globalization which does not require breaking ties with one's homeland, as was the case a century ago.

Simon Kim has done us a great service in focusing attention on the lens that will be needed to view the immigration from Asia in its distinctiveness and its complexity. Although numerically much smaller than the immigration from Latin America, it is linguistically and culturally much more complex than its Latin American counterpart. It also has a notable feature for understanding the future of American Catholicism: it provides a disproportionately higher percentage of clergy for the Church than other cultural populations.

By inviting us to focus on the Asian immigration and its implications for the US Catholic Church, Kim introduces and sheds important light on significant issues that will have to be taken into account in shaping the pastoral response of the Church to its own members and in its mission to the larger society. First of all, he proposes a different kind of narrative than the traditional one. He notes the convergences of significant dates that will shape this new story: the 1964 Civil Rights Act, the 1965 Hart-Celler Act, and the 1965 close of the Second Vatican Council. These provide both the wider societal context for understanding the current immigration as well as the impetus for a transformed Church, more engaged with the world around it. He suggests that we examine and compare what he calls pre–Vatican II and post–Vatican II immigration. This imaginative act will help attune the immigration narrative to both the continuities with the past and also the distinctive features that the immigration of the current period entails. He offers the convergence of these three events as the field in which the Holy Spirit is working and compares it thoughtfully with what the early Church had to confront in the Jew-Gentile question that it took up at the Council of Jerusalem.

Second, Kim looks at three of the most significant groups coming from Asia—from Vietnam, from the Philippines, and from

Korea. He not only looks at the sheer numbers and the distinctive histories of each group but also offers a theological reading of what special gifts each group brings to the US Church. This moves his account beyond demographics and cultural history to the questions of what their distinctive experiences will mean theologically for the US Church, not only in its pastoral response to its members, but also to its missionary outreach. In so doing, he lays the groundwork for developing pastoral policies that will be more attuned to the genuine spiritual and pastoral needs of the United States today and in coming years and not be simply a replication of what has gone on before.

Migration is one of the salient, uneven unsettling, dimensions of life on this planet today. At this writing, Europe is experiencing the greatest movements of peoples since the end of the Second World War. People fleeing violent conflict and persecution, and others seeking a better life for their families, constitute a worldwide phenomenon that every country faces. The relative ease of travel open to at least some of these migrants only intensifies the phenomenon. A one-size-fits-all policy toward immigration and migration in general does not do justice to the dignity of the people involved—both migrants and those who receive them, as well as those who have been left behind. We need investigations that help us reshape the narratives and policies under which we will operate as well as close readings of distinctive peoples and their gifts and the challenges they face. Simon Kim has opened the door on the story of immigrants to the Catholic Church from Asia in a distinctive and imaginative way. And we should be grateful to him for doing so.

Robert Schreiter
Catholic Theological Union, Chicago

Preface

Being intentional is a popular phrase within Catholic circles these days. We are called to be intentional disciples through a discernment process, imitating the Twelve who followed Jesus in the gospel accounts. Rather than passively walking through life—where we knowingly or unknowingly let others make decisions on our behalf or let the daily routines of life take their course as bystanders—God's faithful are called to intentionally imitate the life of Christ. For the immigrant, a minority within church and society, there is another intentional step that is needed—a step of not taking one's identity for granted. Just as there are many challenges to face as intentional disciples, there are equally similar challenges for migrants as they forge an identity by incorporating the cultures of their homeland and their new home country.

Therefore, intentional discipleship presupposes that one understands one's identity as a human being and as a child of God. Those in mainstream society are called to focus on the latter, since the former is assumed in the understanding of one's identity by being in the dominant culture. Every decision, however, requires an understanding of oneself standing before the other. As disciples, then, we must be in a position where we know ourselves so that our discipleship involves our entire being. The former, the search for identity, is not a given for many who are immigrants and must undergo a process of reconciling their dual heritage. In this reciprocal relationship, intentionality means that one has an understanding of oneself as a cultural person of faith, while the intentional search for one's identity eventually leads to the foundations of our lives—in particular, our existence in God alone.

In addition to this self-awareness, a greater awareness beyond our own acts must be acknowledged: the intentionality of God. Creation by a simple *fiat* means that the life of the universe has been intentional, especially since there are no accidents with God. More recently, impacting both church and society is the intentional movement of the Holy Spirit. Through the Spirit's prompting, the Catholic Church was able to open her doors to the contemporary world through an ecumenical council, while the United States opened her shores to global immigration through legislative reform. Therefore, the cultural diversity of the United States was not an accidental occurrence but an intentional movement of the Spirit through ecclesial and societal reforms. Through the Spirit's prompting, an intentional world church has emerged in our backyard.

Embracing this ecclesial reality reveals an understanding of the diverse composition of both our church and society as being an intentional movement of the divine. From this knowledge, our actions in the world are reflective of the worship found in the churches. We overcome the fears of living and working with those different from ourselves, since every being manifests the image of God. More importantly, we live out the Gospel message by welcoming strangers and migrants rather than seeing them disturbing our lifestyle. Thus, we work harder than ever to transform our church and society by going beyond our comfort zones and embracing differences as a constitutive way of manifesting Christ in the world. We can only live a life of discipleship out in the world, since the intentional movement of the Spirit is found in both church and society.

Acknowledgments

I am constantly amazed at the people God has placed in my life and the circumstances of our encounter. These contacts have been both fruitful and a great support in all of my endeavors. Long story short, a simple car ride at the airport in San Antonio with Peter Casarella led to an unimaginable relationship with the Center for World Catholicism and Intercultural Theology at DePaul University. At the invitation of William Cavanaugh, I was able to spend fall 2015 in Chicago, an invitation that led to publications, conferences, and, most importantly, friendships. Thus, I am indebted to Peter Casarella, William Cavanaugh, and the CWCIT staff for supporting me not only in this book but also in my life work at the service of the church.

I am also appreciative of the Korean American Catholic communities in Chicago for welcoming me into their churches and homes during my stay in the city. This communal support has been another source of inspiration affirming my pastoral endeavors as well as motivating me theologically. In particular, I am truly grateful to Fr. Pio Kyoung Hwan Yi and St. Paul Chong Hasang Church in Des Plaines for inviting me to pray with such a wonderful community. I was also warmly received by the Yang family who allowed me a place to call "home" while in Chicago. The wonderful people at DePaul and the surrounding faith communities made my time very special, while at the same time, much more difficult to leave. Without the support of individuals, local communities, and institutions, this book along with many other projects would not have materialized.

Introduction

It is amazing how Jesus' simple words from two thousand years ago, "Come, follow me," would eventually lead to the emergence of the world church as we know it today. The gathering of twelve disciples during Jesus' earthly ministry allowed the maturation of the apostles to continue to "bring good news to the afflicted, to bind up the brokenhearted, to proclaim liberty to the captives, release to the prisoners, to announce a year of favor from the LORD and a day of vindication by our God; to comfort all who mourn" (Isa 61:1-2), especially after the death and resurrection of the Lord.[1] From these humble beginnings, ecclesial organization and structures became necessary as communities outgrew their homes and became noticeable mainstays in their society.

In particular, the development of the church was accelerated because of the rapid growth through the addition of members to its fold. The increase in numbers of disciples naturally takes precedence over questions about the racial and cultural identities of those who chose to follow the way of Christ. After all, the Pentecost experience illustrated the cultural diversity of the church's beginnings as "Parthians, Medes, and Elamites, inhabitants of Mesopotamia, Judea and Cappadocia, Pontus and Asia, Phrygia and Pamphylia, Egypt and the districts of Libya near Cyrene, as well as travelers from Rome, both Jews and converts to Judaism, Cretans and Arabs" (Acts 2:9-11) were the first to experience the outpouring of the Spirit. The initial followers of Christ already lived within a culturally diverse society and witnessed the inclusion to their fold of other Jewish people and those who converted to Judaism since "Luke tells us that it was composed of Jewish

believers and carried out its mission among Jews only."[2] The question, however, of whether future conversions of Gentiles to Judaism as prescribed by the Mosaic law were necessary for them to
become followers of Christ would quickly arise with Jesus' command to spread the good news to all nations, especially by the
"more mission-minded" Hellenized Jews.[3]

At the Council of Jerusalem, apostles and presbyters discussed
the need to uphold the Mosaic practice as it became a central concern to the *kerygma*, "the good news to the poor, the blind and the
captive" proclaimed to the Gentiles.

> After much debate had taken place, Peter got up and said to them,
> "My brothers, you are well aware that from early days God made
> his choice among you that through my mouth the Gentiles would
> hear the word of the gospel and believe. And God, who knows the
> heart, bore witness by granting them the holy Spirit just as he did
> us. He made no distinction between us and them, for by faith he
> purified their hearts. Why, then, are you now putting God to the
> test by placing on the shoulders of the disciples a yoke that neither
> our ancestors nor we have been able to bear? On the contrary, we
> believe that we are saved through the grace of the Lord Jesus, in
> the same way as they." (Acts 15:7-11)

The early church concluded that the cultures of both the Jews and
the Gentiles must be respected, especially avoiding any imposi-
tion of one over the other when doing so would hinder believers
from following the way of Christ. Through this conciliar decision,
Gentiles were no longer required to adhere to the Mosaic law;
respect for the traditional beliefs of the Jewish people, however,
should be honored as well, if doing so would not hinder their
discipleship. This compromise resulted from the need to remove
stumbling blocks such as circumcision while at the same time
preserving aspects of the Mosaic law that the Jewish Christians
could not relinquish in their own approach to God.[4] In short, the
council removed what would keep Gentile Christians from the
breaking of the bread as Christ commanded while preserving
the Jewish purification rituals as needed for this table fellowship.

The prohibition of eating non-kosher food needs to be seen as a reminder for non-Jewish Christians to be sensitive to Jewish scruples but not as an effort to absorb them into Jewish culture and tradition. For the early church, to have common meals was an essential aspect of church life. If this table fellowship was going to survive, Gentile believers would have to respect the Jewish concerns about purity upon which their cultural and national identity in a Diaspora situation depended.[5]

Although the early church resolved the issue of diversity and cultural differences with a compromise that allowed everyone involved to be able to partake at the eucharistic table, the questions raised by the spread of Christianity are still a concern of the modern church. While the spreading of the message of good news to other cultures perpetuates the interest of inculturation in diaspora, the movement back and forth in today's global migration creates a similar concern at home. For example, permanent immigration and transnational migration has created a diverse cultural and ecclesial mix. Therefore, questions about inculturation regarding the faith in diaspora abound outside the United States as well as in the churches in our backyard. Diaspora is no longer "somewhere out there" that foreigners migrate to but is here in our own neighborhoods, as the once monolithic cultural pockets in cities throughout this country have been influenced by people from diverse cultural backgrounds settling in next door. Thus, the US Catholic Church faces questions similar to those that were raised at the first council in Jerusalem over two thousand years ago.

Strategies about the direction the Catholic Church in the United States should take regarding the complex cultural situations created by human movement across the globe abound. One solution is to maintain the existing parochial structures, waiting for the immigrants' next generation to assimilate into the English-speaking liturgies just as in the European immigration experience. This passive response does not answer the cultural questions raised by differing cultural groups of the same faith. At most, this outlook only delays dealing with the similar challenges of the early church that continue generationally. While the European immigration experience in the United States resulted in differing European groups becoming a homogenous worshiping community, this development occurred with the end of linguistic and biological differences as well as ongoing European immigration to the United States. Even with global migration at its height, with "South-to-South" migrants as numerous as "South-to-North" migrants, European immigration to the United States has become almost nonexistent as Western and Central Europe went from a continent of emigration to one that is now a continent of destination.[6]

Immigrants from other areas of the world have not been afforded the same opportunities as their European counterparts, both in terms of being able to blend in as a homogenous group because of the complexity of the current racial mix along with their desire to retain their cultural and linguistic heritage. In addition, immigration has not dissipated as it did in Western and Central Europe, even when the country of origin has vastly improved its their standard of living, a result of the transnational movement created by a global economy. Therefore, the concerns of the early church regarding cultural accommodation are pertinent for the immigrant faith as well as for the existing ecclesial organization.

Churches throughout the world are facing similar scenarios as diaspora exists out there as well as in our backyard neighborhoods. Questions about cultural inclusion and respect for the existing faith culture exist today more than ever and continue as a major contributor of the faith. Therefore, church leaders are wondering what the best course of action is in dealing with a world church in our backyards; do they allow ethnic churches to meet the needs of the initial immigrants and their offspring, or do they merge different cultures into a single multicultural worship space? The solution to put off any major commitments until the next generation does not move the church forward, as the early church illustrates. Only by dealing with the cultural challenges of a world church, especially in our backyard neighborhoods, does the church find her mission as demonstrated at the Council of Jerusalem.

The cultural diversity within the Jewish people, and more so in the encounter with the Gentiles, was not accidental as the pouring out of the Holy Spirit on people from various regions as well as Jesus' command to go to the all nations indicates. Likewise, the world church, not only in the diaspora outside but also in the diaspora inside our neighborhoods, exists by the same movement of the Holy Spirit as a continuation of the faithful fulfilling Christ's mission. The reaction (or lack thereof) of many parishes and dioceses across the country make it appear that the diversity of our communities and churches were either occurrences without any warning or emerged haphazardly and almost by accident. The ecclesial and social events of the 1960s, however, were inspired by the Holy Spirit, thereby transforming the US church and society through the coming together of differing ethnic groups.

The cultural complexity found in the United States today resulted from the social developments of the 1960s, in which the civil rights movement sought equality for everyone regardless of skin color. This equality eventually led to other movements or struggles for recognition and to be counted as one among equals. In particular, the brutality of white Americans toward the nonviolent protesters during the civil rights movement opened the hearts and changed the mind-set of an entire nation. This acknowledgment that all peoples are created equal allowed for legislative changes to the immigration laws of the United States. Previously, only a handful of select countries from Europe with similar faith professions were allowed to enter the "land of opportunity." Quota systems excluded those who were "different" from coming to the United States. Only after the equality won through the civil rights struggles did the whole nation entertain the idea that this country should allow immigrants regardless of race, gender, or religious profession, as immigration reform focused primarily on family reunification.

The first half of this book examines the social, political, and religious transformations that took place in the 1960s. In particular, 1965 was filled with the inspiration of the Holy Spirit as witnessed in the close of the Second Vatican Council, which opened the doors of the Catholic Church to the world, especially other cultures. Without the vision of Pope John XXIII in calling for the twenty-first ecumenical council, the Catholic Church would never have truly understood the cultural encounters of the early church. In rediscovering her ecclesial nature, Vatican II recognized the need for cultural engagement in her evangelization efforts. Thus, a mind-set of a world church emerged from the conciliar debates. No longer was the Catholic Church about her European features; all cultures were to be respected, as Vatican II highlighted the cultural contribution of every faith encounter.

In 1965, the Spirit was also working in the United States as this country sought a more just and equal society. The passage of the Immigration and Naturalization Act of 1965 (a.k.a. the Hart-Celler Act) allowed for greater numbers of immigrants from all over the world to land on US shores as the prejudicial quota system was abolished. Through immigration reform, equality for all people beyond the confines of US segregation was being realized. Impoverished immigrants from all over the world, along with refugees from war-torn regions, were now able to migrate and begin calling this country their home. These two events in 1965 allowed for a world church to emerge in our backyards.

The second half of the book examines three Asian immigrant faith groups in the post-1965 immigration era. Because of the nature of their departure after the end of the Vietnam War with the fall of Saigon in 1975, Vietnamese American Catholics have an experience of leaving their country similar to the journey found in the exodus account in the Old Testament. Through the examination of their faith journey as Boat People, the biblical notion of promises made by God's people gains more significance in recalling God's faithfulness in keeping the covenant of old.

Filipino American Catholics have modeled an ecclesiology for resettlement in the past, through the lives of their saints, and in the present, through their own immigration faith experience. Their saints were martyrs who were also migrants in their own right as they traveled with the religious to other countries. While living abroad rather than in their own home country of the Philippines, their willingness to model the faith in a foreign country reveals the value of carrying one's faith on the migrant's journey. In addition, the challenges of presenting their cultural heritage as needing a distinct worship space was difficult, since Filipino immigrants speak either English or Spanish or both. Their flexibility and willingness to engage other cultures, however, offers us an insight into the early church, where cultural compromise and respect for the existing church allowed Filipino Catholics a way of participating in both realities.

The Korean American Catholic presence represents how one particular ethnic group has benefitted from the 1965 immigration legislation with its emphasis on reuniting families. The rupture in memory, however, both historical or as a metanarrative, poses a challenge since, through these memories, both identity of culture and faith are transmitted. The compromise at the Council of Jerusalem was an embrace of a new cultural identity that did not destroy previously important aspects of both the Jewish and the Gentile cultures. Through this new ethnic-religious identity, the transmission of the faith became a feasible task to all nations. Therefore, the Korean American Catholic experience reminds us of the importance of storytelling and the need to remember to preserve both a cultural and religious heritage. At times, these two are so closely intertwined that they cannot be separated.

It is my goal that readers will see the historical and ecclesial developments as one movement of the Holy Spirit. The world church we are witnessing in our own backyards in this country is not an accident but truly a gift of the Spirit. Earlier, the question of whether we should promote ethnic or multicultural churches was raised. There are no easy solutions to this question, but our efforts in attempting to respond to this challenge are just as crucial. Rather than taking a passive stance, buying time to simply maintain the existing structure, both models of churches must be supported. Ongoing immigration will ensure the continued demand for ethnic churches, while the diversity of parochial boundaries will naturally lead to a multicultural experience. Thus, both are necessary in signifying that we are continuing to live out the lessons from the Council of Jerusalem. By compromising and promoting both ethnic and multicultural liturgical spaces, the local churches are not only respecting the cultural dimensions of our faith but also removing any hindrances from coming together at the eucharistic table of our Lord.

Chapter 1

Important Themes of the Second Vatican Council (1962–1965)

Foundations for the Local Church

The Second Vatican Council (1962–1965) became an ecclesial event like no other when Pope John XXIII called for the twenty-first ecumenical council shortly after his election as Supreme Pontiff on January 25, 1959. Previously, such gatherings of church leaders formed when there were either doctrinal disputes or other church matters that threatened the unity of the faith. In this case, neither of these situations existed in the church, so the call for an ecumenical council created "unneeded" confusion in the minds of some. Despite the healthy status of churches in Europe and North America, the "good pope"—as John XXIII is fondly referred to—saw the need for internal and external renewals in his prophetic understanding of the church's engagement with society. Even with the unexpected invocation for the council, and without fully understanding the procedures or ramifications from such a gathering, the council fathers came together unified by the call for renewal. Such unimaginable harmony in renewing the church at its outset, however, would splinter by the close of the council four years later, due to the struggles of how to interpret and implement the teachings of Vatican II. Nevertheless, some important lessons that are necessary for the church's ongoing engagement

1

of the world can be gleaned in the initial unity and enthusiasm in renewing the church.

Challenges in the reception of Vatican II after the close of the council, and for us still today, do not diminish the importance of themes and movements from conciliar debates and final drafts on the impact and development of the local church. Prior to Vatican II, a European model of church life was upheld as exemplary for the faithful everywhere. While this gave Catholics in other parts of the world a systematic approach to learning and practicing the faith, this approach seldom recognized the need for the church to respect and engage other cultures. Such acknowledgment and embrace of others, however, are truly necessary components of furthering our understanding of God's economy, since a deeper awareness of the incarnation continues to unfold through every aspect of the human encounter. Thus, the Second Vatican Council began to move in the direction of recognizing differing cultures and peoples as also being part of God's plan of salvation. As conversations of a church in the midst of the world gained momentum, the council fathers discovered the need for linguistic and cultural adaptations while attempting to address the characteristic of the majority of the world's population as the church of the poor.

Church in the World and Not the Church and the World

From its inception, Christian thinkers have struggled with two worlds—the kingdom of God and the kingdom here on earth. In the New Testament, St. Paul describes this tension between the two worlds intimately, even relating to an individual's spirit embattling with the flesh: "I say, then: live by the Spirit and you will certainly not gratify the desire of the flesh. For the flesh has desires against the Spirit, and the Spirit against the flesh; these are opposed to each other, so that you may not do what you want. But if you are guided by the Spirit, you are not under the law" (Gal 5:16-18). St. Augustine's *City of God* further highlights the distinctions between the City of God and the City of men. Reacting to pagan worship, St. Augustine illustrates two societies to distinguish between believers in the realm of God and unbelievers in the sphere of men. Evidently, the relationship between the heavenly and earthly kingdoms has been a *quaestio disputata* ever since for theologians trying to reconcile human activity with God's grace. A dualistic temptation to separate the two worlds and only long for the kingdom of God during our earthly existence is a strong attraction, while considering the earthly kingdom as a heavenly reality has been a difficult task throughout history. Although there are two realities, this does not mean that there are two histories— church history versus earthly history. Rather, both societies are encompassed in a singular timeline as salvation history. The task then is to understand the necessity of both in fully bringing about the reign of God while at the same time not reducing or collapsing these two realities into each other.

Prior to the Second Vatican Council, the Catholic Church was entrenched in an isolated position that failed to fully recognize this constitutive relationship between the earthly and heavenly realms. The inward focus created a hierarchy longing for the past where the Catholic Church enjoyed not only political power in conjunction with the state as the two became literally synonymous with each other but also longed for the time when the Catholic faith was not divided by the Reformers who sought to return to the ways of the faithful found only in Scripture. Thus, the distancing memory of this *ancien regime* led the church to retreat into a *societas perfecta*. In the process, it alienated the world and made it irrelevant in the life of the church. Prior to the council, the church firmly established herself as a *societas perfecta* in reaction to both the divisions within Christianity and the development of civil society without any religious influences. In doing so, the Catholic Church defined her existence as a "perfect society" possessing "all that was necessary for the achievement of this society's particular end, namely the salvation of souls."[1]

This ecclesial concept was not new but can be traced back to the patristic period that gained momentum after the Reformation and reached new levels after the emergence of a civil society void of religious affiliation.[2] As is often the case, reactions to heretical notions of the faith entrenched the church into the mind-set of a *societas perfecta*. Reactions to the Augsburg Confession, the

Anglican Branch Theory, and fundamentalists who claimed the church of Christ existed in all Christian denominations rather than in just one denomination, all contributed to strengthening the Catholic claim of an independent society thwarting whatever would weaken the church's influence in people's daily lives.[3] "Moreover, because it was the visible structures that were under attack . . . theologians focused their efforts on [legitimizing] the Church's institutional structures."[4] The safeguarding of the faith in this manner, however, distanced Catholics from any interactions with people of different political and religious thought. In turn, this led the Catholic Church to see herself containing all the truths required to be human while neglecting the fact that humanity has only one history and is continually enriched by the encounters with others.

The consequence of such a reaction distanced the church not only from seeing the Spirit at work in the world but also realizing that the world contained the Spirit just as she did—the church became lost behind the walls of pseudoperfection and independence. Thus, the fathers at the Second Vatican Council attempted to acknowledge that the world is necessary in fulfilling the church's mission to spread the Good News of salvation by reengaging the two societies in God's reign. By opening her doors to the world, the Catholic Church entered into dialogue with the surrounding civil and religious structures. This dialogue was made possible in part by an understanding that while the church has traditionally taught the world, the church can also learn from the world, since the Spirit is active in both. In truth, learning was not the only thing at risk of being lost. At stake was the truth that human encounters are necessary to allow revelation to unfold throughout history. Since divine revelation is God's communication to humanity, every human encounter provides an occasion to deepen our understanding of the divine. In short, discussions from the opening to the closing of the council revealed that a new way of approaching the world was needed.

This pressing concern was also raised in Vatican II's final document, *Gaudium et Spes*, since throughout the conciliar debates the engagement of the world became a central issue and impacted the overall renewal of the church. Some resolution to the question of the nature of the church's relationship with the world came in the opening sentence where the council fathers addressed the world in a positive light. This concluding document was a development of all four sessions of the council (1962–1965), as the distinction between the earthly and heavenly realms needed to be distinguished. At the same time, this distinction needed to resist the prior temptations of falling back into a complete separation. Therefore, the question asked at the council revolved around the relationship between the two—do we speak of this relationship as the "church and the world" or as the "church in the world." The former still had a lingering connotation of separation that the church was trying to resist, while the latter recognized the world as an intimate part of the salvation process. Led by the Spirit, the council fathers concluded that the world and the church were not two entities able to exist apart from one another, but rather, that these two distinct worlds were interconnected. Therefore, the heavenly city is realized in the earthly city and not just a distant reality that will come one day as implied in the title of the only pastoral constitution, *Gaudium et Spes* (The Church in the Modern World).

Promoting a World Church through the Vernacular

Although the Second Vatican Council did not discourage the use of Latin, the church's mother tongue, the council fathers understood the need for the use of the vernacular or the native language when it was appropriate in evangelizing differing cultures and peoples. *Sacrosanctum Concilium*, the first of sixteen documents of Vatican II, addressed this need of being able to utilize the language of each locale in order to encourage the laity to fully and actively participate in the life of the church.

> But since the use of the vernacular, whether in the Mass, the administration of the sacraments, or other parts of the liturgy, may frequently be of great advantage to the people, a wider use may be made of it. . . . These norms being observed, it is for the competent territorial ecclesiastical authority . . . to decide whether,

and to what extent, the vernacular language is to be used. Its decrees have to be approved, that is confirmed, by the Apostolic See. Where circumstances warrant it, it is to consult with bishops of neighboring regions which have the same language.[5]

Therefore, the ability to pray in a familiar language was seen as indispensable for the spreading of the faith in the modern world. The council fathers believed that linguistic comprehension was necessary for the laity and even for the clergy for full and active participation in the liturgical life of the church. Another consideration for the vernacular that would emerge in the postmodern world was the need for further linguistic distinctions between cultural groups beyond just the familiarity with the language. Since evangelization and outreach involve devotional practices or popular religiosity in addition to sacramental practices, particular nuances of the vernacular must also be respected. While the third translation of the English missal implemented in November 2011 attempted to unify the English-speaking countries into a singular linguistic form, this uniformity was shortsighted, as it did not fully recognize that devotional language of the local people needed further distinctions.[6] The liturgical life is "closely related to culture, and, as a culturally-related mode of communication," it cannot be confined to a single linguistic expression based on a particular context.[7] Rather, liturgy must evolve with the people's use of communication, not as a way of letting go of the past, but as a way of embracing, preserving, and building on the rich heritage of prayer. The intention of the council fathers to allow for the vernacular was to determine local customs in linguistic expressions in order to highlight the embrace of the universal faith.

The spread of the Catholic faith in the vernacular helped promote the world church discussed at the council through the incorporation of cultural nuances found in the language of the people's prayers. These linguistic adaptations also carried with them a cultural way of understanding and living out the faith. By encouraging the use of the vernacular, the council allowed a world church to begin emerging based on distinct cultures from each locale. The vernacular opened the way for the laity to participate more fully and actively in the life of the church and symbolized the emergence of the world church that was no longer solely based on a European context, even though allowing this heritage to emerge within a different context would not be an easy task. In some missionary territories, religious and laypeople working on the front lines of developing the local church were already doing whatever was necessary for the faith to embed in the new conditions encountered. In some ways, Vatican II was the seal or formal recognition of what was already happening in the mission fields.

> It was this document which, for Protestants no less than for Roman Catholics, opened the door to the positive re-assessment of "inculturation." Inculturation is the process by which the Gospel is expressed and lived within particular cultures, and *Sacrosanctum concilium* applied this principle to the reform of the liturgy, insisting on a deep respect for the many different cultures that make up what Karl Rahner called the "world Church," and authorized the adaptation of the liturgy to the "native temperament and the traditions of peoples." It even acknowledged that in some parts of the world a "more radical adaptation of the liturgy" may be needed.[8]

Upon the fiftieth anniversary reflection of *Sacrosanctum Concilium*, reports from differing parts of the world agreed on the many gains that emerged from this constitution, including increased involvement of the laity as well as other advancements of church life.[9] Some unfinished tasks of incorporating the vision of the church at Vatican II, however, included congregations still not being real liturgical communities as minimalistic practices, heavily relying on rubrics, continued.[10]

> We have accomplished liturgical reform but not yet liturgical renewal. The dimension of mission is missing, and our celebrations do not reflect the reality of the lived experience of our people. We have put all our eggs into the "Mass" basket. We have not looked seriously at a plurality of liturgical provision, and the overlarge number of "Eucharistic Services" and their obsession with "getting" Communion threatens to derail attempts to broaden the base. We need genuine non-eucharistic and non-sacramental

forms of worship that draw people in by their very attractiveness. This is particularly true in the area of rites of passage and of opportunities that do not yet exist, such as liturgies of grieving or even anger.[11]

This reflection on the fiftieth anniversary of *Sacrosanctum Concilium* does not minimalize the importance and the centrality of the Eucharist for Catholics; rather, the critique further emphasizes the need for local expressions of the faith to be cultivated so that in the harvest, the encounter within the Eucharist will be more fully realized. In other words, how we get to the Eucharist is just as important as the encounter with the Eucharist, since without the former, the entering into the deeper mysteries of the Body of Christ cannot occur. Distinguishing cultural nuances in the vernacular is more than just about an appropriate or acceptable translation. Rather, these local expressions are the seeds of faith for greater participation in the sacramental life of the church.

A current and interesting example of this reality is found among the recent converts to the faith in the Korean Catholic Church. The growth of the Catholic Church in Korea is not due to the emergence of the next generation as the country as a whole is declining with unprecedented low birthrates. Rather, the increase of church membership is due to the older generation of nonbelievers who contemplate their eternal destiny and in particular, the nature of their departure from this life. The Catholic Church in Korea can be said to be more Roman than Rome, at times, as Roman Catholic structures and practices have been implemented with precision over time. The funeral liturgy, however, is one example of a case in which the Roman Rite has not necessarily trumped the local customs but has, in fact, found a truly symbiotic way of coexisting. Thus, the prayers for the dead (*yeondo*), which go beyond just the eucharistic celebration with its incorporation of chants and prayers following a cultural timeline, look and feel Korean within an ecclesial atmosphere of the church. This combination was an organic development of the local faith community and is now very attractive to those considering joining the church. The vision of the council fathers at Vatican II could not have envisioned particulars such as the development of the funeral rite in the Korean Catholic Church; their openness and attitude toward the world, however, opened the doors for the local church to create such prayers to bring the faithful to the eucharistic celebration of the entire church.

There are other factors, such as the influx of migrant workers who are primarily Catholic, that account for overall church growth. The attractiveness of the Catholic faith to Koreans, however, stems from familiarity with overall cultural aspects of Korean life. In addition to the Catholic funeral rite, the hierarchy resembles that of a Confucian society, while vows such as poverty or leading a simpler way of life are ideals that can be upheld regardless of religious affiliation. These cultural nuances embedded in the Catholic Church in Korea are, knowingly or unknowingly, attractive elements in the evangelization and growth of the local church. What resulted out of the missionary practices during the first half of the twentieth century, out of necessity and then was acknowledged at the Second Vatican Council, truly gives life to the church today.

Collegiality and the Laity

The abrupt end to the First Vatican Council (1869–1870) due to the outbreak of the Franco-Prussian war left many to wonder if Vatican II was just a reiteration of the unfinished council or if the second ecumenical gathering at the Vatican almost a century later would go beyond the papal-centric tendencies of the first. One sign that the Second Vatican Council would not be just a repetition of the First Vatican Council or previous ecclesial thought was that at the onset of the council, the fathers rejected the preparatory documents that were intended for discussion. Instead, they wanted to embrace this opportunity to discuss the same topics with openness and freedom. This flat-out rejection of the initial schemas revealed the unity of the majority of the council fathers and that this ecumenical gathering would be more than just the continuation of Vatican I. The near-century that passed from the first to the second ecumenical council provided ample time for the council fathers to comprehend the need to promote and broaden the identity and mission of the church while still adhering to past practices.

An example of this adhering and advancing of the church in terms of its structure can be found in the document on the church, *Lumen Gentium*. Within the document, the bishops speak of collegiality and their own role in union with the pontiff. Just as the universal church represented by the papacy was fully evident, the local church with the bishop as its head also contains the fullness of the church. Therefore the bishops of the world in union with the pope held the apostolic succession of servant leadership.

> Collegiate unity is also apparent in the mutual relations of individual bishops to particular dioceses and to the universal church. The Roman Pontiff, as the successor of Peter, is the perpetual and visible source and foundation of unity both of the bishops and the whole company of the faithful. Individual bishops are the visible source and foundation of unity in their particular churches, which are modelled on the universal church; it is in and from these that the one and unique catholic church exists. And for that reason each bishop represents his own church, whereas all of them together with the pope represent the whole church in a bond of peace, love and unity. (LG 23)

The renewed emphasis in *Lumen Gentium* on the role of bishops allowed Catholics to look to their ordinary, and not just Rome, for guidance in their daily spirituality. By doing so, *Lumen Gentium* further promoted a world church since it further highlighted the distinctiveness of each individual diocese around the world.

Within the vision of a church in the modern world, collegiality becomes important as the centralization of any organization cannot exist without local stability. With the stress on the individual in postmodern thought, collegiality can become more confusing; it is, however, even more necessary than ever before. While Vatican II may have spoken about the role of individual bishops within their own dioceses and how they come together as a college through the apostolic succession, the council does not address the issue of migration, in which people from dioceses halfway around the world come to settle in new locales. The connection to one's homeland is neither lost in resettlement nor are the ties to the local church back home severed. Rather, the complexity of immigration allows each believer to have access to the local church in their country of origin and destination, further intensifying the universal aspect of the faith. Therefore, collegiality becomes even more crucial, since the juridical authority to shepherd one's flock is not confined to just the local diocese, as bishops from all over the world must work in conjunction with the movements of their people to ensure spiritual guidance everywhere. An example of this complexity is found in the Korean American Priest Association where the bishops' conferences of both the country of origin (Catholic Bishops' Conference of Korea, CBCK) and destination (United States Conference of Catholic Bishops, USCCB) are involved in the pastoral care of Korean American Catholics.[12]

As collegiality in *Lumen Gentium* sought to connect the Bishop of Rome with his brother bishops around the world, it also sought to find a rightful place for the laity. Previously, the emphasis on liturgical participation was mainly focused on the episcopacy or the presbyterate. The council fathers, however, understood the invaluable asset of the laity and the necessary implementation of their gifts and talents as the church progressed forward. "All the laity, then, have the exalted duty of working for the ever greater extension of the divine plan of salvation to all people of every time and every place. Every opportunity should therefore be given them to share zealously in the salvific work of the church according to their ability and the needs of the times" (LG 33). Thus, the emphasis on the laity came with their call for "full and active participation" going beyond the liturgical celebrations. The laity were now seen as a necessary and vital part within the entire life of the church.

In the case of the Philippines, the increased involvement of the laity has resulted in a greater equality between the sexes. Prior to Vatican II, the emphasis on the hierarchy promoted a male-centric participation within the church. The emphasis on the role of the laity has increased women's presence in the church, but a divide still exists in some minds because of the nature of ministries. The integral role of the laity within the Filipino people's matriarchal structure (rather than patriarchal, which is common in other Asian countries), however, has fostered a sense of equality, perhaps more so than in any other country. Rather than being a situation where women feel excluded in the church (although some tensions still exist), the directives of Vatican II have reinforced the maternal aspect of Filipinas.

As liturgical celebration involving more and more of the laity supports the overall cultural context of the Filipino people, their involvement also lends itself to the development of their theological or spiritual outlook. For example, Filipinos' portrayal of Mary as the Mother of God emphasizes the maternal needs within the encounter with the divine, both in church and society. In addition, their spiritual approach based on these maternal characteristics allows for a gentler pastoral approach in ministry. This does not mean that every need is met or that everyone feels the kind of warm embrace they have received from their own mother when they come to church. Lay involvement, however, has been much less divisive than in other countries where issues of gender and sexuality have been more heavily skewed throughout history. Being matriarchal, Filipino society has allowed increased lay participation after Vatican II to bring greater equality to the roles of women and men in the church of the Philippines.

This call for the laity to fulfill their baptismal promise also became evident in the immigrant church as the laity were often the first to gather their community members and provide the bulk of the labor in initiating a process to gather communities in diaspora. Unlike the early immigration patterns of the United States, where clergy and religious often followed the faithful in their immigrant journey, the post-1965 immigrants often resettled in the United States without such spiritual guides in their community. Therefore, the call for the laity to embrace every aspect of church life without the sacraments was evident in the creation of ethnic faith communities across the nation. Often, the laity were the ones to establish enough of a sense of a community and later invited necessary clergy and other personnel to more fully develop the church today.

The drive of the laity in developing their faith communities within their immigration process went beyond the scope of *Lumen*

Gentium but suggested why the laity had a central role in being church. Beyond the sacramental practices of these immigrant faith communities, the laity were often the creative ones in finding places for worship, integrating as best as they could with the English-speaking communities in the United States as well as finding alternative ways of preserving their cultural religious heritage once a community reached a certain level of maturation. Often this would eventually lead to a request for a priest and religious from their homeland for the ongoing pastoral care of these immigrant communities.

Catholic Social Justice in Solidarity as the Church of the Poor

A theme that was discussed but never really emerged at Vatican II was for the people of God to be the church of the poor. Poverty was an important issue for the "good pope," as he spoke about a church of the poor in his speeches leading up to the opening of the council in 1962. This topic, however, never emerged on the council floor partly because John XXIII decided not to intervene in such matters and partly because of the fact that bishops from the First World did not truly understand the poverty that ravaged the Third World. Therefore, only in hallway discussions between breaks did some of the council fathers understand that a world church would have to take on the characteristics of the majority of the faithful whose lives were in the midst of this difficult and impoverished situation.

Questions after the death of Pope John XXIII at the end of the first session immediately arose. With the passing of the pontiff, would the ecumenical council continue, or would one session be enough? Also, would the church return to her inwardly ways, or would she continue in engagement with the world? After all, the entire purpose of this ecumenical gathering was not always clear, even during the first session. The unfortunate passing of John XXIII left not only the Second Vatican Council in doubt but also the direction of the church, especially in her relationship with the world. The question was simply put, "Are we going the way of Peter or the way of Paul?" meaning, is the church focusing only on herself or will she go out into the world? With the election of Cardinal Montini and his choosing the name of Paul VI, these concerns were quickly addressed. Pope Paul VI would continue on the path of his predecessor.

During the conciliar activities of the next three years, Paul VI was able to promulgate constitutions, decrees, and declarations of the Second Vatican Council, placing the church on a path of internal and external renewal. In addition, Pope Paul attempted to also raise the consciousness of the church as being a church of the poor. Through his own acts of solidarity, the pontiff's actions on behalf of others afforded the church an opportunity to pause and reflect on the poor. One of his most notable acts of humility as Holy Father was to surrender the papal tiara on the altar of St. Peter in 1963 as a gesture of giving up the riches and privileges in both church and society that the papacy once sought. The tiara would not be worn again by any pope, since it appeared contrary to the Gospel message and the church's vocation to the world. A simple gesture, with many implications, as the engagement with the world was no longer about control and authority symbolized in the ornate headgear. Engagement with the world would now be about appealing to the masses, those filling the pews and those on the streets, the often neglected and overlooked poor in society. In 1964, Pope Paul made another notable act when he donated his limousine to Mother Teresa on his visit to Bombay, India. The limousine was sold in a raffle and the proceeds went to her ministry caring for the lepers on the street. Mother Teresa received more than a fourfold return than the value of the vehicle, and with it, she built a home for lepers.

Paul VI will probably be best remembered for continuing the Second Vatican Council after the death of John XXIII and his later encyclical, *Humanae Vitae* in 1968, which addressed the controversial subject of artificial birth control. His legacy, however, should also include the continuation of John XXIII's desires for the church. He, as with anyone holding this office, is a reminder of how to live as a "Servant of the servants of God"—one of the eight titles for the papacy.

After the close of the Second Vatican Council, the concern for the poor would be much more vigorously taken up by the people of Latin America. Through the bishop's conference (CELAM), theologians, pastors, parishioners, and the poor themselves, the emphasis on a preferential option on behalf of those living in poverty would emerge and become a central theme in Catholic Social Teaching. The historical developments within church and society following the council, with its emphasis on the poor throughout the world, further confirm the conciliar activities of Vatican II and the necessity of the church's engagement of the world.

Chapter 2

On the Fiftieth Anniversary
of *Gaudium et Spes*

The Movement of the Spirit in the Church

*The joys and the hopes, the grief and the anguish of the people of
our time, especially those who are poor or afflicted, these are the
joys and hopes, the grief and anguish of the followers of Christ as
well. Nothing that is genuinely human fails to raise an echo in their
hearts. For theirs is a community of people united in Christ and
guided by the holy Spirit in their pilgrimage towards the Father's
kingdom, bearers of a message of salvation for all of humanity. That
is why they cherish a feeling of deep solidarity with the human race
and its history.*

> *Now that the Second Vatican council has studied the mystery
of the church more deeply, it addresses not only the daughters and
sons of the church and all who call upon the name of Christ, but
the whole of humanity as well, and it wishes to set down how it
understands the presence and function of the church in the world
of today. (GS 1–2)*

Just as one may embrace *Gaudium et Spes* with "joy and hope,"
like the title of the final conciliar document at Vatican II denotes,
others may consider the pastoral constitution from the council
fathers with as much "grief and anxiety." This dichotomy found in
the opening sentence of the final document, promulgated the day

before the close of the Second Vatican Council, is a stark reminder of the division in the document's reception concerning how best for the church to enter into a healthier relationship with the world. In fact, *Gaudium et Spes* was critically analyzed from every stage of its development since it was initiated during conciliar debates at the opening session—rather than from preparatory drafts—and thus, the council fathers debated it to the very end. From the opening session of Vatican II, the fathers felt the need for the church to reverse its previous posture toward the world by engaging it in a positive manner. Thus, "Schema XVII" was included at the end of the first period and the beginning of the intercession period within the number of shrinking decrees to be debated. The persistence of this theme of engaging the world survived because the majority of the council fathers understood that a new relationship was needed between the church and the world. The ongoing debates regarding this draft evolved into "Schema XIII" after undergoing numerous revisions and then was eventually promulgated as the only pastoral constitution at the Second Vatican Council.

The ideas in paragraph 39 of *Gaudium et Spes* solidified the council's desires to engage the concerns of the world for the growth of the human family. While embracing a close relationship with the world, the church still insisted on distinguishing these two realities and not collapsing or reducing the church into the world or vice versa. "That is why, although we must be careful to distinguish earthly progress clearly from the increase of the kingdom of Christ, such progress is of vital concern to the kingdom of God, insofar as it can contribute to the better ordering of human society" (GS 39).

The new vision regarding the encounter between the church and the world, however, fell into criticism from the very beginning of the conciliar debates. From the start, the council fathers were concerned with the amount of importance that the world should be given within this engagement. As the pendulum swung, propelling the church out of isolation, the council fathers were tempted to see the world containing "all that was necessary" for salvation. This extreme view from the other end of the spectrum, however, created an alternative *societas perfecta* of the world and did not represent the relationship that the council fathers intended. At times, it appeared this was the direction the Vatican event was headed as the momentum caused by this overdue emergence from isolation catapulted the church toward the world with an optimism regarding humanity's potential. Thus, it is easy to see why people criticize this relationship for its problematic extremes, eventually collapsing the isolating mentality of a *societas perfecta*. When the council tried to balance the relationship between the church and the world, there arose further criticism, as "the words *church* and *world* were used indiscriminately, without proper attention to their different meanings"—further exacerbating the problems in defining this relationship.[1]

In addition to the vagueness of what the council fathers meant by the terms, other issues plagued the schemas, making those at the council cautious about approaching the world with such openness.

> Two other general concerns were, first, whether the right balance had been achieved between the vocation of people in this life and their eternal or eschatological calling, between the natural and the supernatural; second, whether there should be more concentration on the church's teaching or, rather, on "signs of the times." Both concerns reflected, in different ways, tension between "from above" and "from below" approaches.[2]

Still debating about the encounter between the church and the world, some wanted to begin with the perspective of the church while others wanted to start with the perspective of the world. This was not a new dilemma but a debate lasting throughout church history, especially discussions that involved realizing the humanity and divinity of Christ. Coming out of the *societas perfecta* fortress, the council's instinctive tendencies were either to embrace cautiously this newly envisioned relationship from the church's perspective of eventually moving out to the world or to plunge enthusiastically into this dynamic interaction of seeing the world containing similar qualities as that of the church. The notion of placing the world on the same level as the church raised many gut-level reactions and eventually divided those involved with Vatican II and throughout the council's reception afterward.

The criticism of "naïve optimism" regarding the attitude that overvalues the world was based on the view that the world was capable of bringing about a better reality, let alone salvation, on its own. In particular, the desire to approach the relationship "from below" with the world was heavily criticized because of a lack of a theological understanding of sin in the world by those who overvalued what the world could do on its own. Aspects of this criticism leveled at the final document of the Second Vatican Council severely divided theologians who were once so unified at the beginning of this historic event just four years earlier. Sin, or the lack thereof, in the final text became an obstacle in fully embracing *Gaudium et Spes*, reflecting the uneasiness of defining the relationship between the church and the world. The schema regarding the necessity for the church to engage the modern world was, however, not derailed by these shortcomings. Rather, the urgency was greater than the shortcomings, especially as they were running out of time with the close of the council in sight.

A Consubstantial Relationship

> The boldest approach was struck by Bishop Tenhumberg, auxiliary of Münster (Germany). The church, he said, should acknowledge that in the past it had often been blind to the signs of the times or very slow to recognize them. . . . To prevent this occurring again, various things would be needed: a renewed theology of the life and working of the Holy Spirit in the church; a return to the model of authority in the church exercised by Christ, his apostles, and the Fathers, so as "not to extinguish the Spirit but to test all things and to hold on to what is good" (1 Thess 5:19-21); a new appreciation of the charisms and gifts of the people of God. Above all, a new style of authority in the church was necessary.[3]

Conciliar decisions regarding the opening of the church to the world revealed certain blind spots of the past—the church could not entirely eliminate this limitation in moving forward. The desire to see the "signs of the times" was not enough without a proper understanding of how the Spirit was present and active in both the church and the world. Rather than seeing the world as a dangerous place, an attitude prior to Vatican II, or the world now as the same as the church, a temptation during and after the council, Vatican II revealed a relationship between the church and the world as one of mutual necessity. The church and the world are connected through a reciprocal relationship in which the church, to be church, requires the events of the world. Worldly events allow the church to develop her Gospel call for evangelization, as these developments are constitutive to what it means to be church. Moreover, the world is in need of the church for the message of the Good News and salvation. Marie-Dominique Chenu—a French Dominican theologian who was actively moving the church's thinking forward before, during, and after Vatican II, calls this connection between the church and the world a "consubstantial relationship," in which the church derives her being from this vital interaction because the Spirit's involvement in both allows human beings to be in the one history; thus, a "consubstantial relationship" is formed.[4]

Seen in this light, the church and the world are not equals, as some critics claim in their charge of "naïve optimism." Rather, the relationship indicates that the world needs the church for salvation, since history is a singular human event, and the church needs the world in order to recognize her role throughout salvation history through worldly events. Based on Chenu's understanding of the relationship between nature and grace (which involves the idea that the church and the world cannot be separated) and his incarnational approach (in which the church needs to be both present and engaged with the world), Chenu views "redemption as the recapitulation of all things in Christ, including the physical universe and the embodied spirit of man."[5]

By acknowledging the relationship of the Holy Spirit in communion with the Father and the Son in the Holy Trinity, Denis Edwards reveals how the Spirit becomes evident not only in the Pentecost event but also from the beginning of creation.[6] In fact, without the Spirit, there is neither creation nor existence. For God breathes the Spirit into all of creation, giving life to the world. Therefore, all of creation, not just human beings, bear the Spirit. In assigning the proper place to the Spirit, Edwards implies that creation, including the incarnation, involves the Spirit's initiation. Just as Christ is seen as the savior of the world, the workings of the Spirit must also be recognized, since creation is a constitutive aspect of the salvation process.[7]

The relationship of creation and salvation parallels or implies a similar relationship between the church and the world. The "naïve optimism" leveled by critics of *Gaudium et Spes* is only realized when the world is seen as capable of salvation on its own. Therefore, the proper relationship of the second and third persons of the Trinity illustrates that the world is not capable of salvation on its own and only in communion can Christ and the Spirit do what they were sent to do by the Father. Likewise, the church in communion with the world and vice versa brings about redemption and salvation. Just as Christ taught that apart from Him we cannot do anything, the church apart from the world and the world apart from the church falls short of the intention initiated by both the creation and salvation process.

This intimate and necessary communion found in the Trinity is what Chenu is referring to when he places the church and the world in a "consubstantial" relationship. In brief, what gives life to the world is also what gives life to the church. Therefore, the existence of both is found in the Spirit, and although the church has a deeper understanding of the intention of the creation and salvation process, the church does not hold this awareness exclusively. This is what I believe the council fathers were referring to in the drafting of the final document—they were attempting to give the world a proper place in the process of salvation history. Not that the world could bring about salvation by simply bettering itself but that the church apart from the world cannot fully reap the fruits of the Spirit. "Naïve optimism" could be overcome through the proper placing of these relationships based on the trinitarian notion of communion.

The absence or underestimation of the Spirit's presence in all of creation easily leads one to view the world as dangerous and/or irrelevant to understanding the mystery of God. Another critique of *Gaudium et Spes* is the lack of sin. After all, the Genesis account reveals a story of creation involving the Spirit hovering over the waters of chaos as well as being breathed into the life of the first humans. In addition, the Genesis account is also very important in understanding humanity's separation from the intention of creation and thus, the need for salvation. Just as the Spirit is seen alive in both creation and humanity, sin caused by the fall of humanity continues through both as well. Thus, not only is the world in need of redemption from sin but also the church as well. Not only does sin continue in creation but also in the church, since the church is made up of humanity that God has called together. The church is also in need of redemption, but the difference and advantage perhaps is that the church recognizes this need for redemption more so than the world.

At Vatican II, the council fathers saw the world optimistically in a reaction to the *societas perfectas* that closed off the church to others. The breakthrough from this isolation came when the fathers saw the same goodness of the church operative in the world. Likewise, the council fathers failed to identify the complex dimensions of sin in the world because of the speed of being catapulted out of a *societas perfecta*. In essence, the church at Vatican II was looking through a mirror as she viewed the world as she viewed herself. The failure to temper the optimism of what the world could do was possibly attributed to the lack of sinful reality within herself, a mind-set of perfection still lurking as blind spots for the church, even during the breakthrough moments of the Vatican II event. In reality, we know that sin exists in both church and world, and thus, the need for salvation is never in doubt. By acknowledging, however, that both church and world are in need of this saving grace, we once again highlight the Spirit's involvement in both realities.

Thus, Chenu's reflections on the relationship of the church and the world found in *Gaudium et Spes* help us go beyond the initial criticisms and stalemate. By maintaining the church and world engaged in a "consubstantial relationship," Chenu helps us to see that the two cannot be distinguished in such a way but must be maintained in communion with each other since the Spirit is the source and life of them both. Through this communion, the church is in need of the world and the world is in need of the church. Without each other, salvation history is incomplete, as humanity's perfect union with Christ cannot be fully realized. This realization is not just a task of church but can only be realized through the communion with the world. In other words, the church identifies the Spirit in the world while the world gives the opportunity for the church to do so.

At the Pentecost event found in the Acts of the Apostles, the universal church was formed in a localized manner as a diverse group received the outpouring of the Spirit. The universal church came into existence through events in the world. We must ask ourselves what these diverse men and women were all doing in one place. What political and social events were happening that brought these people together and allowed the local church to come into existence? Just as worldly factors contributed to the local reality of the universal church, the Spirit continues to move in a similar manner. The activities of the Spirit in the world highlight the activities of the Spirit in the church, since the church and the world must be in communion with one another for the universal and local churches to manifest. Thus, the periods both leading up to and after the Second Vatican Council parallel the movements of the Spirit inspiring society in a specific manner. In particular, the Spirit's urging of the hearts and minds of people during the civil rights movement, along with the passage of the 1965 US Immigration Act, are worldly factors paralleling the developments of Vatican II in allowing a local church or the further expression of it to be realized in the US Catholic experience. Without the political and social developments of equality, the ecclesiology of Vatican II would not have developed into the local expressions found in the United States today.

Although the Spirit's prompting can be seen in church and society, the council fathers could never have imagined what would occur after the close of the council. A couple of factors contributed to this inability, since the "signs of the times" that were so heralded at the council came with some unanticipated blind spots. For the Catholic Church in the United States, the first blind spot of the bishops resulted from the lack of acknowledgment of what the Spirit was doing in their own society in terms of civil rights and race relations. Their own condemnation of racial injustice was evident in their responses (*vota*), or rather in the lack of thereof, prior to Vatican II and at the council itself. In the United States, discussions concerning race relations began to surface during the late 1950s, revealing that the South was just as segregated for Catholics as it was in the rest of society; only twelve US bishops (8.1 percent), however, "proposed that the issue of race be included in the conciliar agenda."[8] Some individual bishops, such as Bishop Joseph Rummel in New Orleans, actively sought to desegregate Catholic schools in their dioceses; Bishop Rummel was by far the most adamant that Vatican II discuss matters on race relations.

> Rummel pointed out how racism contradicts the doctrines of creation and redemption and asked the Council to bear witness again to their truth. This should include a rejection of all forms of segregation on the basis of race and any kind of efforts to deprive people of their legitimate aspirations. . . . Rummel had encountered bitter opposition when he condemned school segregation in 1953 and again in 1956. In the summer of 1957, Catholic laymen opposed to racial integration had written to Pius XII to challenge Rummel's authority on the matter.[9]

Joseph Komonchak cautions those trying to interpret the US bishops' *vota* with the absence of certain issues as the disinterest or indifference of US bishops.[10] The lack of a unified voice against the injustices that consumed an entire nation, however, seems difficult to simply overlook. While international issues plaguing the world, such as communism, garnered the attention of the bishops worldwide, here in the United States the nation's attention was also riveted on the civil rights movement. Therefore, the miniscule amount of *votas* raising the issue of an injustice gripping the nation's consciousness is difficult to reconcile as anything other than indifference toward the movement. At the very least, it seems that the US bishops were noncommittal on the appropriate response to the situation as indicated by the lack of unified support for the civil rights movement.

In addition to the blind spot resulting from political, economic, and social situations, another blind spot emerged afterward, this time involving the council fathers and the reception of Vatican II.

The inability for the wider church to recognize the "signs of the times" should not be attributed to the ignorance or lack of concern of some individuals. Rather, because Vatican II addressed the modern world and could not envision the postmodern realities to come, the council's ecclesiology would be incomplete. Vatican II saw the world in a modern sense and described herself as a world church (or at least emerging to become one) because of the diversity of its faithful all over the world. This world church was called so because the Catholic faith was now represented by members throughout the world and not strictly in a European manner. The gathering of over two thousand bishops from across the globe was a reflection of the world church proclaimed by bishops and theologians alike. The world church, however, was understood as churches all over the world, but a church "out there," not occupying the same spaces geographically. In the postmodern world of migration and globalization, the world church was no longer a reality "out there" in different parts of the world. Rather, the world church would be coming to backyards and neighborhoods of societies that were culturally homogenous. Global migration increased to the United States and other developed nations for those seeking a better life, but this human movement also increased to underdeveloped areas as nations sought to reap benefit from resources found in those impoverished countries as well. In essence, the world church that was proclaimed at Vatican II would evolve into a migrant church as immigrants from all over the world came to call places like the United States their home. The realization of this local church could not have occurred without the political and social developments in the United States and elsewhere during the 1960s.

Just as social and political developments brought people together at Pentecost over two thousand years ago, the social and political developments of the United States brought people from all over the world. Without the urging of the Spirit in the world, the local church in the United States would never have come about as we know it today. Because of these "blind spots" at Vatican II, however, the US church could not have imagined such a development and continues to stumble and grow in embracing such developments in the local faith communities. Without seeing the developments of the world as also the movement of the Spirit, the continuation of the local expression of the universal church is often misunderstood or simply overlooked. Only in seeing the "consubstantial" nature of the church and the world will the local faith communities be truly acknowledged and given their proper place within the universal church. Stated another way, the local expressions are found within the events of the church and world, and without a proper recognition of this communion, these local expressions are not seen for how they contribute to the universality of the Catholic faith. Even worse, we lose sight of the Spirit's working in allowing the Body of Christ to be fully manifested within her members.

Two of the "signs" that were missed or not properly addressed at the council were to become foundational events in the US ecclesial landscape. The failure to recognize these two "blind spots," one occurring in their midst and one on the horizon, did not prepare the US church to necessarily welcome or embrace the local faith communities found today. Although certain measures in recognizing different ethnic faith groups through refugee relief services did aid in the resettlement process, these measures did not necessarily give these new ethnic groups a chance to share their gifts of faith in the existing local churches or in the wider community.

As previously stated, the emerging local church after the Second Vatican Council and the passage of immigration reform in 1965 was a direct result of the Spirit's working in the church and society. First, the struggles of the civil rights movement paralleling the development of the council was not strongly raised by the US bishops with a unified voice before and during conciliar floor debates. Second, the modern world, which was evolving into a postmodern reality with its global migration, created a stage that the church could never have anticipated at the council. The former was an oversight by the US bishops for not taking the civil rights movement as a serious movement of the Spirit, while the latter was something the entire council could not have imagined as a "sign of the times."

The developments in the United States during and after the council illustrate this "consubstantial relationship." An example is the civil rights laws eventually leading to the passage of immigration laws respecting differing peoples. This development, both political and social, would serve to change the population landscape of not just civil society but also within the church. Without civil rights and immigration movements, the growth of the US church would not have occurred as immigration has been the factor in allowing the church to maintain or surpass other religious institutions in overall population. The inability to see the Spirit working in these movements makes these historic events a nonfactor in the ecclesial life of the US church.

If we account for sin, then not every historical development is a movement of the Holy Spirit. Therefore, discernment is always a priority, since sin is present in the world. Regardless, every historical event does affect the church in some manner, and an ecclesial response is always required. The council fathers attempted to anticipate this scenario through their debates on culture. In a humble gesture, the council fathers recognized the consequences of leaving their past of a *societas perfecta* by also relinquishing control of their cultural surroundings. "There was general agreement that the topic was important and must be covered in the decree; there was also agreement that the church was no longer in control of culture, as it has been in times past, at least in Western Europe."[11] Thus, this surrender allowed the possibility for a relationship to emerge between the church and the world. For the US Catholic Church, the political and social developments of the 1960s created a world beyond the realization of the council fathers. But by opening her doors to the world, the church accepted this possibility and must now respond to worldly events that move us forward. The desire to go back to the *ancien regime* or any aspects of the previous world prior to the Second Vatican Council is not realistic now that the doors have been opened. By acknowledging cultural developments outside her control, the church, in essence, revealed why the world is "vital" for the kingdom of God.

In the United States, the "signs of the times" of the civil rights movement capped by the Civil Rights Act of 1964 and the Immigration and Nationality Act of 1965 propelled the local church in a vastly different direction. Today's tension with local ethnic communities of faith still revolves around the reconciliation of the US church before and after Vatican II. There is a real tension between the Euro-American immigration experience of the past with the post-1965 immigration experience. But there is abounding dialogue as well.

The 1965 immigration legislation altering the discriminatory practices toward East Asia changed the social and ecclesial landscape of the country. The growth of the US church has been attributed to immigration, with Hispanic/Latino immigration being the main contributor.[12] The Hispanic/Latino people existed in the United States prior to the Immigration Act—they were already present in the southwestern region of this country and did not necessarily present a new challenge for the local church. The Asian influx, however, created a noticeable diversity in the fabric of ecclesial life. With their presence, the world church with her diversity, previously witnessed only in the homeland of each country, is now becoming a reality in the United States.

The Second Vatican Council and the US Catholic experience illustrate the presence and movement of the Spirit in the church and the world. These two movements affirm the council's work in *Gaudium et Spes* and also with the entire ecumenical council. The "vital" relationship between the church and the world is necessary for complete redemption, since the Spirit is active in both the church and the world. Without these simultaneous movements, the local expressions of church evaporates into the universal, and the interchange between the church and the world does not always elicit an ecclesial response. *Gaudium et Spes* not only opens the doors to the world but also requires active participation and interchange between the two for the church in the world to be realized.

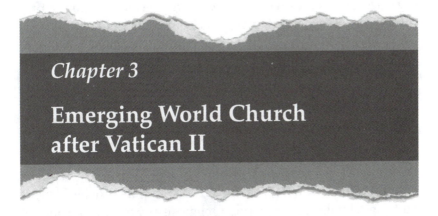

Chapter 3

Emerging World Church after Vatican II

Conciliar Reception in the Korean Catholic Experience

Attendance of Korean Bishops at Vatican II

Like many Asian bishops, the Korean episcopacy favored a progressive outlook at the Second Vatican Council in order to reconcile social and religious differences in society.[1] These same bishops, however, steadfastly held on to a conservative reading of Scripture and understanding of revelation, since they held as a priority the safeguarding of the faith.[2] Their voting patterns were not self-contradictory but highlighted the fact that they were indeed responding to their socioreligious context. On the one hand, by voting conservatively on revelation, the non-native bishops from Korea were preserving what was handed down in faith. On the other hand, by voting progressively on religious practices such as Marian devotions, the bishops were able to reconcile some of the cultural, social, and religious differences between church, society, and other religions. The move toward cultural embrace and ecumenical outreach allowed for Catholic appeal to the wider population as the faith resonated with social conditions. The voting pattern of the Korean bishops reveals the ongoing mission in the transmission of the faith by emphasizing the cultural realities back in Korea.

One reason Vatican II was so influential in renewing the world church was the way the progressives were able to mobilize and organize themselves. The bishops from Asia sided with the progressive groups, since they responded most closely to the needs of the church back home. By participating with those residing at *Domus Mariae*, the bishops from Asia were able to partner with their counterparts from other continents in the hopes of renewing the church through cultural and social engagement.[3] In Korea, conciliar renewal allowed Catholics to engage the democratic movements in politics and the struggle for economic prosperity after the devastation of the Korean War, better their relations with Protestants (who came to be the majority of Christians), dialogue with Buddhists who were once seen as a hindrance to the Catholic faith, and, finally, accept popular religiosity by reconciling ancient practices such as ancestor worship with recent liturgical renewals. In summary, Vatican II allowed the Catholic Church in Korea to come into dialogue with society and thus to become a more credible witness in its social, economic, and political developments and less antagonistic to other religious practices, especially since Catholicism was the religious minority.

In Korea, Vatican II reforms did not have the immediate and widespread impact that they had in Europe or North America. One explanation for the differences in reception in Korea versus in the West is the fact that the council fathers who were spearheading floor debates were primarily from Europe or North America. Thus, the renewal that emerged was originally directed to their concerns. Even with the Korean bishops in attendance, the reception of Vatican II back home was not as dramatic as it was in the West for several reasons. First, Catholicism in Korea was not as developed as in the West, as the entire country just survived the devastation and poverty of the Korean War and, therefore, was not focused on the same social concerns. Next, Korea was a mission territory where many of the structural renewals and practices discussed halfway around the world did not necessarily apply or were already being creatively implemented according to the needs of missionary conditions. Finally, the documents of Vatican II took nearly five years to be translated into Korean. Therefore, the reception of Vatican II is quite complex and still being lived out in different parts of the world, including Korea.

Similar sentiments were echoed by the retired bishop of Incheon, William McNaughton.[4] Bishop McNaughton went to Korea as part of the Maryknoll mission in 1954. He was installed as the bishop of Incheon in 1961 at the age of thirty-four. In addition to being at all four sessions of the council, Bishop McNaughton oversaw the reception of Vatican II during his episcopal tenure in Incheon that lasted forty years. Being an American missionary in Korea provided Bishop McNaughton a unique perspective on the Second Vatican Council. On the one hand, he could relate to the floor debates, having been educated in the United States. On the other hand, he understood that the cultural context of Korea was vastly different from those of his Western counterparts and thus, reception took on a different understanding and timeline. The Korean Catholic Church had to adapt to limited resources, much like the nascent Korean church of the nineteenth century, because of its vast mission territories and recovery from the devastation of the Korean War. Pastoral adaptations such as the vernacular liturgy (progressive translatability), while maintaining the tenets of the faith (conservative mission) discussed at Vatican II, were already being incorporated from the 1950s on an as-needed basis for a developing church and society.

In addition to being a developing nation (in contrast to the influential countries at Vatican II), Korea did not experience such dramatic changes after the council due to its Confucian roots. Rather than the individualistic ideals of the West, the family-oriented social and religious structures in Korea allowed for a more gradual implementation of conciliar teachings.[5] Because of Korean's Confucian ordering of society, the churches in Korea were more cautious and thoughtful in the implementation of Vatican II. Like many nations that are still uncovering the richness of Vatican II and deepening their understanding of it among an increasing Catholic population and increasing resources, Korea is still attempting to live out the conciliar lessons and is reaping the benefits of this ecclesial event.

Although the Vatican II event may not have had an immediate impact on Korea in the 1960s, the overall renewal of mission and translatability of her ecclesial nature allowed the Catholic Church to develop in unison with the growth found in the rest of society. Thus, Vatican II propelled the church into the social and political struggle of a developing nation. In the second half of the twentieth century, the church supported the democratic movement of Korea, and many protestors found safe haven at the Myeongdong Cathedral in Seoul. In addition, Catholics began to engage society by building schools, hospitals, and other institutions that benefitted society at large, a work that was previously neglected in the first half of the twentieth century. Thus, the translatability of spreading the good news by social engagement was not necessarily in words only, but more importantly, in actions directed toward people in times of poverty and in people's struggle for democracy.

While the sentiment of lifting the whole country after the devastation of war fueled the unifying cry of the nation, Vatican II, in many ways, helped amplify this cry by altering the previous ecclesial outlook and steering the church to engage society in its religious and social developments. The lessening of social and religious distinctions between church and society found throughout the conciliar documents was an important step in revitalizing the church, especially in this part of the world—the development of an impoverished country was neither strictly a religious nor a social cause. Rather, the unifying endeavor to better conditions was a socioreligious movement where the translatability of the faith implicitly was being lived out by the faithful engaged in society.

The Nature of the Korean Church: Incorporating the Vernacular

A revolutionary moment at Vatican II was when the council fathers decided to allow local churches to use the vernacular to increase the participation of the laity. "Full and active participation" became the popular mantra as the faithful's liturgical engagement would be complemented with their engagement in society. Just as the council sought to enlarge its structural understanding as a *communio* relationship of the faithful, council fathers acknowledged the *sensus fidelium* of the laity and thereby recognized the Spirit's work in both the faithful and eventually the world.

The use of the vernacular moved the Latin-speaking church to engage other cultures throughout the world. Rather than insisting that all liturgies be conducted in a foreign language in a Tridentine manner, Vatican II moved the faithful to worship in a manner that reflected their natural expressions of faith. In Korea, the vernacular liturgy not only helped develop local faith expressions but also made the acceptance of others easier. For example, *Legio Mariae* (a Marian devotional imported from Ireland), the charismatic renewal from the United States, Marriage Encounter from Spain, *Focolare* (a movement for unity) from Italy, and small base communities from Latin America—these liturgical prayer groups are prime examples of how the vernacular directives of Vatican II allowed the faithful on the Korean peninsula to incorporate their own linguistic expressions with those of the universal faith.

Another example of translatability in the Korean acceptance of the faith is the unique *yeondo* prayers in the funeral rite. While adopting the Latin burial rite, Koreans have retained certain elements of their cultural prayers that were used prior to receiving the Catholic faith. Thus, *yeondo* has ancient cultural overtones that have been incorporated with the litany of saints and maintains the timeline derived from the indigenous understanding of the spirit world. By recalling the saints in the Catholic heritage along with deceased loved ones, the Korean faithful found a way to reconcile the Catholic honoring of saints with their obligation to honor ancestors.

The missionary zeal of Vatican II allowed for translatability to go beyond just the vernacular as ecclesial structures were also transformed, since *lex orandi, lex credendi* meant that the church prayed what she believed. In particular, rigid parochial structures gave way to small, base communities as hierarchical models gave way to communion models. Vatican II saw the need to uphold every member of the church and approached the relationship between the clergy and laity in a cell-like *communio* model, upholding the institutional and communal aspects of the faith.[6] In the Korean experience, small communities of faith emerged in the ecclesial landscape, encouraging local communities and laying the foundation for rapid church growth.

Activity of the Church: Struggle for Democracy

Perhaps the greatest contribution the council made to the Catholic faith in Korea was its encouragement to engage all aspects of society. The renewal *ad extra* of church allowed Catholics not only to embrace political struggles for democracy but also to reclaim their rightful place as a people of faith actively engaged in society as first witnessed by the Korean Martyrs. The retreat from society during the turn of the twentieth century, influenced by French missionaries, limited social engagement and thus growth of the church even after many lives were sacrificed for the faith. "The Korean Catholic Church's traditional framework of separating religion from politics, which had been introduced through heavy influences of French missionaries," was redacted by the Second Vatican Council, especially in promoting "the dignity of the human person and the common good in social and political spheres."[7]

> With the paradigm shift in worldview, the Korean Catholic Church has shown a remarkable growth not only in demography but also in evangelical activity in the public realm of the Korean society. The Church has actively participated in solidarity actions for the marginalized, and protested against dictatorial governments for democracy's sake. As a result, the Korean Catholic Church came to gain the greatest credibility among all religions in Korea in 2008–10.[8]

Later realization of conciliar teachings can be attributed to the lack of religious crisis Korean Catholics faced compared with their counterparts in the West. For example, issues about religious life for women only emerged after the numbers of women in religious life peaked in the 1990s, when religious orders faced similar issues of the West such as the decline in the number of candidates along with aging members. Only after such population development did a new direction for women religious, based on the Vatican II's vision of renewal that addressed the current climate, begin to emerge (a translatability of religious life for Korea).[9]

Cardinal Stephen Kim Sou-hwan (1922–2009) was the archbishop of Seoul for thirty years and a fierce social justice advocate in Korea's struggle for democracy and modernization. Having been originally ordained a bishop of Masan in 1966, Cardinal Kim was a product of Vatican II and embodied the conciliar spirit of renewal throughout his episcopacy. Two years after the council, Cardinal Kim asked a series of questions of why Vatican II was needed and if the call for internal and external renewals were truly understood.[10] He maintained that the liturgy had changed only passively and "full and active participation" called for in the church's renewal was not embraced because the faithful did not truly understand that internal reforms needed corresponding external renewals through engagement with society.[11] Thus, Cardinal Kim's call for renewal through the study of Vatican II corresponded with the completed translation of each document by the end of the decade. Rather than limiting the interpretation of conciliar teachings to only Church "elites," such as bishops and theologians, he thought the laity in mutual cooperation with the clergy should be called on to help the local church realize the renewal called for by Vatican II.

In addition to challenging the faithful to study Vatican II, Cardinal Kim's outspoken criticism against the military dictatorships of the 1970s and 1980s and constant insistence on human rights and the common good endeared not only him but also the entire church to Korean society as a credible witness. By vocally denouncing the imprisonments of protestors and the abusive treatment of its citizens, Cardinal Kim became an iconic figure for resistance and solidarity against corruption. Myeongdong, the cathedral of the archdiocese of Seoul, also became a symbolic place for protest demonstrations and a safe haven for those persecuted. At Cardinal Kim's side were other outspoken bishops, priests, and laypeople whose uncorrupt and just presence gave great credibility to a minority church—a credibility that would attract many to conversion in later years.

Like his contemporary, Cardinal Kim, Bishop Daniel Tji Hak Soun (1921–1993) of the Diocese of Wonju also advocated for Vatican II's call for renewal to be realized within church and society. In 1971, parishioners followed his example of protesting against government corruption in a special intention offered at Mass. This prayer of protest illustrated that the Church was able to identify social issues relevant to the faithful but was not yet mature enough to become the prophetic voice that Vatican II called the church to be in the world.[12] Eventually, the Wonju movement would become the church's wake-up call with the imprisonment of Bishop Soun in 1974 for his constant condemnation of social injustices. Although the documents of Vatican II were translated by the early 1970s, the translatability of the conciliar teachings were just beginning to be realized in sociopolitical discourse with Bishop Soun at the forefront. This struggle for democracy would allow the church to make sense of the Gospel message within the reality confronting the Korean people.

As the church matured with the translatability of the Gospel message in society as promulgated by Vatican II, Bishop Soun's prophetic voice reached its peak in 1977. In a series of lectures, Bishop Soun called on the recognition of the dignity of human persons by considering what constitutes the essence of human beings both as individuals and as communal beings.[13] In addition, Bishop Soun called for the decentralization of both church and society through Roman decentralization toward local bishops, clerical decentralization toward God's people, and Catholic decentralization toward other religions.[14] Centralization, according to Bishop Soun, was the source of injustice for the masses, and the obvious solution was a decentralization in which the people should be trusted to lead whether in church or society.

Following these prophetic leaders, many priests also began to study the documents of Vatican II in the 1970s. The inspiration gleaned from the social teachings of the church stirred them to establish associations among the clergy and to encourage the laity to do so as well based on their reading of political, economic, and social "signs of the times" in relation to the realities of the church as called forth by Vatican II. Thus, the entire church in Korea, from top to bottom, was called on to engage in the political, economic, and social development of the country. In anticipation of the two hundredth anniversary of Christianity in Korea, a preparatory committee concluded that the social and pastoral experience of Korea was indeed a creative interpretation and application stemming from Vatican II and subsequent Catholic social teachings.[15]

The Korean reception of Vatican II was truly an embodiment of spirit at Vatican II engaging in renewal of the church in relation to society. Another pastoral committee created for the two hundredth anniversary commented on the implication of mission of the local church and concluded that Korean Catholics reflect the internal and external renewals initiated by the Holy Spirit at Vatican II. This proud heritage would be formally proclaimed in a pastoral statement by the Bishops' Conference in 1982, which culminated with the canonization of 103 Korean martyrs by Pope John Paul II during his historic visit to Korea in 1984.

Chapter 4

On the Fiftieth Anniversary of the 1965 Immigration Act

The Movement of the Spirit in the World

The immigration reform that emerged as legislation in 1965 was not an isolated act but one that developed over time as a reaction to biased immigration practices favoring a handful of countries. In particular, two other historic moments or turning points leading up to the 1965 legislative reform are attributed to the shifting of attitudes of immigrants who were not from certain European Protestant countries. In 1880, the first legislation, which changed previous patterns of immigration from Europe, opened the way for non-Protestant immigrants. The shift in immigration policy allowing for eastern and southern Europeans had two significant impacts in terms of geographic and religious differences as Catholic and Jewish immigrants were allowed to enter the United States. Eventually, the United States limited the influx of these non-Protestant immigrants through immigration legislation in 1924, which would also indirectly impact other ethnic groups regardless of religious affiliation. "The 1924 immigration act, commonly known as the National Origins Quota System, justified discrimination in immigration based on national origin. Thus it severely curtailed immigration from Eastern and Southern European countries and completely abolished immigration from

Asian countries."[1] On the heels of the civil rights movement, immigration policy changed drastically to reflect the equality people gained regardless of their skin color and religious preference. Thus, the 1965 legislation focused on reuniting families, providing opportunities to those whose occupational skills were in demand, and offering safety to political refugees.

The Immigration and Naturalization Act of 1965 opened the door for immigration to all countries by abolishing discrimination based on national origin. More significantly for Asian immigration is that the new immigration law abolished "Asiatic Exclusion," which had eliminated Asians based on a quota for nearly forty years. As a result, the new immigration law has encouraged immigration from non-European countries, particularly from Asian countries. The number of immigrants from Asian countries has seen dramatic gains since the enforcement of the new immigration law. The proportion of Asian immigrants increased from 9 percent in 1960 to 25 percent in 1970 and 44 percent in 1980 (Immigration and Naturalization Service 1960, 1970, 1980).[2]

As with any legislative reform, immigration and naturalization reform had its share of supporters and critics inside political circles or within the sphere of public opinion. Debates about whether or not to open the United States to increased global immigration centered on previous biases in immigration reform, the consciousness of equality raised from the civil rights movement, and/or future implications of population growth as the consequence of an influx of non-European immigrants. Even with suggestions of such sweeping reforms, still others felt that the change in immigration legislation would lead to little or no impact on overall society. One such important figure during this whole legislative process was President Lyndon B. Johnson, who considered the passage of the Immigration and Naturalization Act, known as the Hart-Celler Act, as a symbolic gesture when he signed the immigration legislation bill on October 3, 1965.

Addressing the crowd at Liberty Island in New York, President Johnson remarked, "This bill that we will sign today is not a revolutionary bill. It does not affect the lives of millions. It will not reshape the structure of our daily lives, or really add importantly to either our wealth or our power."[3] This shortsightedness resulted from his reflections of past biases that needed to be addressed by his experience of current events. His own struggles with and alongside the civil rights movement during his administration revealed the need not only to fight current social injustices but also to correct the wrongs of the past. Therefore, rather than seeing the passage of the immigration and naturalization legislation as impacting the future direction of the country or perhaps using the moment to calm people's fear of unknown immigration possibilities, Johnson focused on correcting the wrongs of the past and balancing the issues of equality raised by Dr. Martin Luther King, Jr. and the civil rights movement. Thus, immediately after remarking about the "nonrevolutionary" nature of this legislation reform, Johnson commented, "Yet it is still one of the most important acts of this Congress and of this administration. For it does repair a very deep and painful flaw in the fabric of American justice. It corrects a cruel and enduring wrong in the conduct of the American Nation."[4]

Equality and justice for Johnson was not just about fairness for those allowed to immigrate to the United States. He also took into consideration the unfair practices and prejudicial bias of existing immigration laws with the following statement:

> This bill says simply that from this day forth those wishing to immigrate to America shall be admitted on the basis of their skills and their close relationship to those already here. This is a simple test, and it is a fair test. Those who can contribute most to this country—to its growth, to its strength, to its spirit—will be the first that are admitted to this land. The fairness of this standard is so self-evident that we may well wonder that it has not always been applied. Yet the fact is that for over four decades the immigration policy of the United States has been twisted and has been distorted by the harsh injustice of the national origins quota system. Under that system the ability of new immigrants to come to America depended upon the country of their birth. Only 3 countries were allowed to supply 70 percent of all the immigrants. Families were kept apart because a husband or a wife or a child had been born in the wrong place. Men of needed skill and talent

were denied entrance because they came from southern or eastern Europe or from one of the developing continents.[5]

Johnson's focus and emphasis on family reunification instead of the separation of peoples because of race, color, creed, or place of birth went against the core of America's past understanding of immigration. Johnson said, "This system violated the basic principle of American democracy—the principle that values and rewards each man on the basis of his merit as a man. It has been un-American in the highest sense, because it has been untrue to the faith that brought thousands to these shores even before we were a country. Today, with my signature, this system is abolished."[6]

Obviously, Johnson was thinking about the present and the past and not the future implications of his signing into law the Hart-Celler Act when he echoed the words that ended so many other injustices in the world—the abolishment of slavery as the prime example that comes into the minds of the people in this country. "To abolish," however, has a stronger connotation than just stopping a practice previously done before. The word itself comes from Latin, *abolere*, which means to completely destroy or cause to no longer exist. Therefore, the abolishment of the previous quota system of immigration was an acknowledgment of not only a prejudicial system based on race but also a privilege—"twin barriers" that Johnson felt hindered the country from recognizing the beauty and strength of how immigration was the origin and the foundation of this country. The president proclaimed, "Our beautiful America was built by a nation of strangers. From a hundred different places or more they have poured forth into an empty land, joining and blending in one mighty and irresistible tide. The land flourished because it was fed from so many sources—because it was nourished by so many cultures and traditions and peoples."[7]

Ironically, the country's attitude toward immigration reform sparked similar debates that we still encounter today. Those fearful of a future with peoples and cultures who are foreign to themselves often resort to recounting stereotypical accounts of dangerous situations involving these foreigners in our midst. Included in these fear-driven accounts is the portrayal of how the nation becomes weaker because of the dilution of a monocultural outlook. Although Johnson did not envision the massive impact this piece of legislation would have on the fabric of American society, he did not fall prey to the fears of his own "prophets of doom" who thought that the prejudicial and privileged quota system provided much more security and strength to the nation than did correcting the errors of the past. Thus, Johnson without knowing what the future would hold from increased immigration, prophetically reminded the citizens of this country that historical development through ongoing immigration made the United States everything opposite of what critics were proclaiming:

> And from this experience, almost unique in the history of nations, has come America's attitude toward the rest of the world. We, because of what we are, feel safer and stronger in a world as varied as the people who make it up—a world where no country rules another and all countries can deal with the basic problems of human dignity and deal with those problems in their own way. Now, under the monument which has welcomed so many to our shores, the American Nation returns to the finest of its traditions today.[8]

The passage of the 1965 Immigration and Naturalization Act ended the superficial immigration policy of appearing to welcome the weak, tired, and those without a home and focused US efforts on unifying families and make better attempts to welcome those in need to call the United States home. The Hart-Celler Act allowed the United States to open her shores to the world in such a manner that changed the social and cultural landscape of this country and is in many ways a standard for other countries witnessing the global migration of the world. Events leading up to the middle of the decade in the 1960s resulted from the end of the Second World War where countries around the world were literally being carved up between the United States and Soviet Union, in what would come to be called the Cold War. The differing philosophy between capitalism and communism of how best to govern, protect, and promote its citizens exploded as territorial disputes throughout the world erupted into tragedy where brothers ended up fighting brothers in civil wars. From the increased violence of these conflicts, migration became necessary for displaced peoples to survive as refugees.

In addition to the Cold War, the economic disparity between the First and Third World further exacerbated the tense situation, leading many to migrate as economic refugees. As colonialism slowly began to withdraw throughout the world because of the civil wars in many of these regions, the absence of this antiquated system gave way to a new form—this time in the form of neoco-lonialism, where corporations sought out cheaper resources of materials and labor to maximize profitability. The replacement of an oppressive political system for a controlling economic system produced similar results as indigenous peoples were displaced within their own countries, leading to further displacement spill-ing over to neighboring regions willing to accept them.

The causes of displacement and migration in the twentieth century need much more discussion than given here; the global conflicts, however, directly or indirectly caused by the United States, afforded this country an opportunity to bring relief to the rest of the world with the passage of immigration reform. After the 1965 Hart-Celler Act was fully enacted three years later, many of the first wave of immigrants were escaping economic or po-litical conditions created by tensions of the Cold War or between First World and Third World economies. Sociologists often call these tensions that lead to migration elsewhere "push factors." These situations "push" or even force people to move from their homelands to other regions for political and economic refuge. Along with these "push factors," there are also "pull factors" that increase migration, although oftentimes the push/pull have some commonalities—either one leading to the other or working in unison. In addition to these "push factors," the "pull factors" often involved certain needs of the United States in the growth of its economy and the care of its citizens, allowing certain skilled professionals to enter the United States. Specifically, healthcare workers were in high demand after the passage of the 1965 im-migration legislation, leading many to come to the United States to offset the shortage of skilled workers.

The Civil Rights Movement and Equality for All in the United States

The connection between the civil rights movement and the change in the US immigration policy in the 1960s is quite simple—without the activities of the civil rights movement and the passage of the Civil Rights Act in 1964, the Immigration and Nationality Act of 1965 (the Hart-Celler Act) may not have been established. Without the call for equality regardless of ethnicity represented in the civil rights movement, the opening of the doors to immigrants from such diverse ethnic backgrounds would have been unfathomable. The 1965 US Immigration Act undid the prejudicial exclusion of some immigrants in general and Asians in particular by allowing families to come to the United States and create a new life in a country originally founded on this model of immigration.

Black struggles against racism in conjunction with the struggles of immigrants impoverished by war and poverty across the globe renewed both church and society as we know them today. Social and ecclesial developments were not accidental or coincidental but rather aided by the Spirit's movement in the world. The Civil Rights Act of 1964 and the Immigration and Nationality Act of 1965 opened US shores to others and made the newly arrived foreigners acceptable (albeit sometimes in very primitive ways, initially) and thus allowed for the emergence of a diverse group of people not only in society but also within the church.

> Just as lightning makes no sound until it strikes, the [revolution for civil rights] generated quietly. But when it struck, the revealing flash of its power and the impact of its sincerity and fervor displayed a force of a frightening intensity. Three hundred years of humiliation, abuse, and deprivation cannot be expected to find voice in a whisper. The storm clouds did not release a "gentle rain from heaven" but a whirlwind which has not yet spent its force or attained its full momentum.[9]

The Spirit's activity in the civil rights movement became evident as proponents who marched in a nonviolent manner, resisting the temptation for revenge, also paused to call on God's strength in the face of brutality.[10] "In the summer of 1963 the knife of violence was just that close to the nation's aorta. Hundreds of cities might now be mourning countless dead but for the operation of certain forces which gave political surgeons an opportunity to cut boldly and safely to remove the deadly peril."[11] Obviously this was not strictly a march of protesters against the oppressors, as marchers also found consolation in these moments of prayerful reflection during nonviolent campaigns. These spiritual pauses propelled marchers to keep their eyes focused on justice and allowed them to endure many hardships along the way. In addition, many churches, spearheaded by their pastors, intimately linked their cause with the social injustices plaguing their communities, the nation, and even the world, as a religious movement strengthened by the Spirit within the hearts of men and women regardless of race and beliefs.

The Spirit's presence also became visible within the movement's preaching, marching, and singing, paralleling a trinitarian movement. Preaching, marching, and singing—our actions in the world—are the communal result of what have been discerned as God's calling in quiet solitude as well as in communal celebrations. Often our energies focus on finding God in sacred spaces while neglecting our solidarity with the poor and oppressed in society as the Spirit's presence in the world. Without this solidarity, the trappings of a *societas perfecta* of praising God in isolation is always before us, for the Spirit calls the church to engage the world through an act of solidarity in a concrete manner.

Preaching, marching, and singing became an intricate part of the fight for civil rights as the black church supplied the "organizational muscle, and Christianity (supplemented with a dose of Mahatma Gandhi's methods of nonviolent protest) supplied the moral and theological capital."[12] The preaching of black pastors in front of congregations reached far beyond the walls of the church. They were heard as outcries against the racial inequality that enslaved entire communities, and they echoed in the hearts and minds of the entire nation, reaching all people regardless of skin color. The blatant cruelty in the way blacks were treated and the failure to recognize the human dignity of God's creation regardless of ethnicity was intolerable to society. The black community could no longer be silent. The preaching of pastors reverberated throughout the landscape as the call for liberation of oppressed people resonated with God's call for all believers. Without the message of liberation from mostly black preachers, the civil rights movement would not have been able to move forward. For it was in their proclamation that minds and hearts were unified. The unifying force of preachers was an important component in realizing the spirituality of the civil rights movement. Their words made real the oppression, struggles, and the liberative action required in living out God's word. The proclamation of Scripture in the midst of segregation made concrete the personal dialogue between God and the oppressed as well as those in solidarity with the Spirit's activity in the world. The preaching of God's liberation in the black community allowed hearers of God's word to participate in nonviolent ways. This participation, initiated by preaching, was the concrete expression of the Holy Spirit.

Men and women came together in solidarity to begin marching against the injustices plaguing the black community and poisoning overall society as preached from the pulpit. This outcome, the way to march in a nonviolent manner, needed discernment through prayer before God, so that the march itself became a prayer before one another. Nonviolent marching with arms locked with one another signaled another spiritual presence as a way of imitating the movement of a liberating God and continuing the work of salvation history. Marching is a spiritual activity, because every footstep is part of the process of liberation. It was not simply an exercise of the body, since the physical activity of moving toward racism, prejudice, and injustice was a participation in the work of the Holy Spirit engaging the church with the world.

Finally, the singing of hymns in the churches where God's word was preached overflowed into the streets during the marches toward people and structures that reinforced racism. Marching is a natural progression from the preaching (the message from the pulpit that demanded social justice) just as singing in praise of God (spirituals that contained the history, culture, and religious expressions) accompanies the marching and preaching.

The melodies rising from the depths of the oppressed, along with those in solidarity, proved to be both the creative expression of the movement as well as the energizing force behind every footstep of marchers, especially when they were fatigued by the journey or wearied by the constant physical and verbal opposition along the way. These voices raised in song continued the example of the Spirit's work in the civil rights movement, for the sadness and painful memories of racism were verbalized in these communal expression of release.

In summary, the spirituality of the civil rights movement was exercised at this particular point in salvation history due to the interior activities of prayer that paralleled the external activities of the church. In addition, the parallels of the contemplative with the active portion of prayer came to become an authentic expression of our spiritual lives because of its liberative aspect. The liberation of blacks required a reevaluation of the structural systems of the United States as well as the hearts and minds of its citizens. The act of preaching, marching, and singing for the liberation of society while overcoming its racial divide demonstrated a concrete relationship of the church and the world, a relationship that failed to resonate with the US Catholic Church (with the exception of some individuals with the courage to be moved by the Spirit in the world).

The Immigration and Nationality Act of 1965 did not have the same dramatic political, social, or religious drama in its inception as did the civil rights movement. After all, this legislative action came at the heels of the civil rights struggles which lasted for a decade and could have only been possible with the equality that was achieved the previous year. In many ways, the 1965 changes to the immigration policy of the United States came as a result of the civil rights movement and also helped further the cause of obtaining people's civil rights by going beyond desegregation alone. Thanks to the struggles of the black community, the rest of world also reaped the benefits of racial equality. Therefore, the Immigration and Nationality Act of 1965 changed the previous quota system that discriminated against some ethnic groups by giving priority to dignified aspects of immigration such as family reunification.

The Immigration Act of 1924 (a.k.a., the Johnson-Reed Act) created a quota system that largely prevented certain ethnic groups such as Asians from entering the United States. With a smack of tokenism, the United States allowed a limited numbers of immigrants. Practicing this discriminating policy, the United States' selective process of who was allowed into the county continued until the 1960s. The Second World War launched the United States onto the international stage, and with that came the need to change some of its previous policies and practices toward those of different ethnicity. Not until the civil rights movement, however, was the United States able to officially change the discriminatory quota system, embracing many who were escaping war-torn and impoverished situations. Not until those of differing ethnicity were seen as equals with those of European descent was the United States able to open its shores to the world.

Chapter 5

Pre–Vatican II Immigration and Post–Vatican II Immigration

An Occasion for Re-imaging the US Migrant Church

Historic markers are necessary for humans to delineate certain milestones as well as dramatic shifts in people's lives. We annually recall these moments through celebrations, memorials, or other traditional ways of recounting the past, whether as individuals or groups. Blowing out candles on birthdays, offering prayers for the deceased on the anniversary of their passing, and having dinners to celebrate wedding anniversaries are just a few of the ways we remember, honor, and celebrate our lives and those around us. As a society in general, there are certain events that are so commonly shared by the masses that they become shared markers for the general population to recall in some emotional manner. A recent event was 9/11, a tragedy that shifted our national consciousness, especially in how we view people different from ourselves. We not only remember the lives affected by this tragedy but also use this date to recall the shifts in this country in our practices, thinking, and outlook. For example, the increased presence of TSA at every airport is a direct result of 9/11. Therefore, people can speak about what security was like "pre-9/11" and compare it to today's "post-9/11" security measures. This is a common reaction in life to create or share distinct historical markers to explain our lives.

49

For Catholics today, the Second Vatican Council has become the historical marker to explain the shifts and revisions in our current Catholic practices. Fifty years later, this conciliar moment still stands as the preeminent milestone for Catholics. No other moment in recent history has captured the entire consciousness of the faithful in its historic gathering of bishops from around the world as well as the sixteen documents produced. Although influential popes, bishops, and other leaders have captured our imagination in one fashion or another, Catholics often speak of church history, practices, and daily life based on the Second Vatican Council. Those who yearn for the days when the church had plenty of seminarians, priests, religious men and women, as well as church-attending parishioners, reminisce of a pre–Vatican II world, while those who embrace the diversity of cultures, languages, and practices among the faithful advocate a post–Vatican II one. Thus, the Second Vatican Council is a historic marker that explains the nature of the church today that changed as a result of the conciliar debates over a half-century ago.

Just by calling for a council, John XXIII created a moment in the church like no other in salvation history and, in essence, a historical marker for the universal church. In the past, councils were needed to clarify doctrinal disputes, political matters, and other church difficulties. The Second Vatican Council, however, was convened during one of the heightened moments of the Roman Catholic Church where there were no expectations for conciliar activities to intervene in ecclesial or worldly matters. The vision of John XXIII went beyond the current events in the life of the world and the church, but this pontiff allowed the Spirit to work through him in calling forth a new era within the Catholic Church. The ability to listen to the Spirit's urging in the world allowed the Catholic Church to move in unison with the changing demographics of the world population.

Even with the Spirit's urgings and the council fathers responding in humility to opening the doors of the church to the world, Vatican II could only respond to the situation from its current or near horizon. Viewing the modern world in hostility prior to the council and then in openness afterward allowed the space for the emergence of the local church. The church, however, even with this unexpected but much needed conciliar event, could not have seen the postmodern state of the world today. For instance, the council fathers understood that their modern reality called for a world church—a church appreciating the diversity of peoples and cultures throughout the world. The postmodern circumstances resulting from globalization, however, became an opportunity for such diversity of both church and society, not only overseas but also in our backyards. The unforeseen human migration allowed the church and society to once again cooperate with the Spirit in responding to the needs of God's people.

Therefore, Vatican II is a historic marker for political, cultural, and spiritual dialogue and thought. In addition, we must remember that in our conversations about immigration, Vatican II also plays an important role. Just as we distinguish a pre–Vatican II and a post–Vatican II church in all areas of ecclesial thought, we must also conceptualize a "pre–Vatican II immigration" and a "post–Vatican II immigration," since the modern and postmodern worlds we live in as church and society were born from the urgings of the Spirit.

Why is it important to speak of a pre– and post–Vatican II immigration? These are terms that are not in our vocabulary, even as Catholics, and yet they are important terms—historical distinctions and paradigm shifts in church and society that must be uncovered today. Too often we speak about immigration and the local church as a uniform or replicated experience throughout salvation history. The reasons for immigration and the formulation of local faith communities, however, are complex, and within each complexity, the ways God calls the church to become incarnate are present more fully. The incarnation at Mary's *fiat* was only the beginning of how the body of Christ would become incarnate in human history. Each moment contains a revelation of divinity and humanity which we must not only preserve and pass on but also cultivate in future encounters between different peoples and cultures.

The terminology of pre– and post–Vatican II immigration is important for today, since these terms refer to specific locales, historical periods, and distinct circumstances that allowed the local church, especially in the United States, to emerge and become foundational institutions within the larger society. Today's encounters with immigration throughout the world have certain similarities but are truly distinct in people and how the immigrant journey forms the people upon their arrival in a new land. In addition, the "lumping" of immigration into common experience does not do justice to the migrants themselves or assist us in understanding God's unfolding revelation through these encounters. Thus, by using terms such as pre– and post–Vatican II immigration, we begin to delineate historical timelines and build on the graces of God's people. If we do not do so—if we do not articulate these specific moments of immigrant history, which is also synonymous with salvation history—then we misunderstand the working of the Spirit at Vatican II and the cultural consciousness raised by the conciliar event. The trouble with the church in the United States is that we do not appreciate how immigration has impacted it, created the foundation for it, and continues to fuel the growth of the church for generations to come. Seldom do we see the church continue to grow generationally without the influx of immigration in both church and society. In not distinguishing the different experiences of immigration, we fail to see the previous experience in all its value and worth; and most of all, we fail to see the importance of succeeding generations of immigrants. The US church often speaks of immigration from its European immigration experience, which reveals the importance for the beginnings of the US ecclesial experience. Within this experience, however, is a complex system of how Catholics from European descent had segregated themselves into national parishes and later generations had merged into a uniformed English-speaking community. This wonderful experience of separate communities becoming one parish cannot be overglorified as a Pentecost experience of how different peoples came together. There are many dynamics, both human and divine, involved in how the US Catholic Church emerged and developed. Also included within these dynamics are the negative experiences of closing national churches once the racial enclaves of the initial immigrants were overcome by the next generations.

The closing of these national parishes, once immigration from Europe began to slow down, caused great distress among the episcopate who oversaw the closure of such communities. The proximity between these national churches, along with the diminishing faithful who needed their mother tongue to participate fully in the liturgical prayers, all contributed to the trauma of closing historical markers that were foundational not only for the initial immigrants but also in building the entire US Catholic Church. This development of the local church from segregated national churches into a uniform parochial entity is a powerful image in the minds of today's church leaders—a foundational image of how the church began but not necessarily how the church should always move forward. In speaking of a pre–Vatican II immigration, the church is able to preserve and honor the Euro-American Catholic experience and continue to build on it. This remembrance, however, is not always one that is replicable, since the context of immigration is vastly different today. For instance, racial and biological similarities allowed for a unified parochial system once the linguistic barriers no longer existed. The similarity of Europeans in creating a Euro-American Catholic experience was a great advantage in the pre–Vatican II immigration experience.

A post–Vatican II immigration speaks about people also coming to the United States seeking better opportunities after the 1965 church and world events. This time, however, the immigration of peoples from all corners of the world created a complex encounter which the pre–Vatican II immigration experience is able to provide some valuable insights in the resettlement but cannot completely address. The modern way of addressing the pre–Vatican II immigration was revolutionary for its day because of the recognition of other cultures contributing to the further understanding of the universal church. The migration of peoples in a postmodern reality, however, creates a complexity of encounters unlike the pre–Vatican II immigration. In the post–Vatican II immigration, we are witnessing the coming together of different peoples in the United States like no other time in American history. The immigration experience after the Second Vatican Council and the passage of the Hart-Celler Act in 1965 allowed another occasion for the local church to emerge by the bringing together of God's people from other parts of the world. The diversity of peoples, unlike the period of pre–Vatican II immigration, cannot simply follow the formulary of church and society found before 1965. In the post–Vatican II model, immigration is continual because of the opportunities and refuge that is found in the United States. Thus, the number of believers who lack similar linguistic and cultural expressions is not declining in the United States but continues to contribute to the growth of the US Catholic Church. Immigration is one of the key components of growth not only in the United States but also in Europe. In addition, the postmodern world affords easy access for immigrants to return or frequently visit their country of origin. The mobility and fluidity of people crossing national and international boundaries contributes to the complexity of postmodern, immigration which a post–Vatican II terminology would begin to identify and address in previously unseen ways.

The post–Vatican II immigration contribution to the local church contrasts with the traumatic experiences of national churches in the pre–Vatican II immigration and continues to illustrate the need for specific places of worship to preserve the cultural and linguistic heritage of the faithful. Where the pre–Vatican II immigration experience created a unified Euro-American Catholic expression, the post–Vatican II immigration experience is creating diverse Catholic expressions that share but continue to develop from the richness of their homeland in addition to the faith found in the United States. Gleaning important lessons from both situations continues to enhance the local churches of the United States beyond just population numbers. The error occurs in expecting the same outcomes of a pre–Vatican II immigration experience. Rather, the pre–Vatican II formulary hinders the development of the local church of the post–Vatican II reality where a formulary is still being lived out. The past can only provide lessons or guideposts as we move forward into the emergence of the local church. Fifty years of experience after the passage of the 1965 immigration laws and the close of the Second Vatican Council have provided time and maturity for these faith communities to begin reflecting on their own experience of departure and resettlement in both church and society.

The inability for us to speak of a pre–Vatican II immigration and a post–Vatican II immigration indicates the lack of understanding of today's global human movement as well as the lack of maturity of faith communities in their resettlement. The resistance to such language reduces human encounters to the past and hinders progress for the local church. Just as we cannot return to a pre–Vatican II world, we cannot continue to meet the needs of those who arrive on our shores within a pre–Vatican II immigration model, and therefore, we must embrace the Spirit's movement of the church and the world in unison. The growth and maturity of the local church, also called the body of Christ, continues to reveal both the humanity and divinity of our Lord. Without such expressions and growth in this direction, the intimacy with our Creator is limited, since all creation includes cultural and linguistic expressions of all peoples. The Spirit's movement over fifty years ago continues to guide humanity's journey toward the divine.

Emergence of a Local Church

While the Immigration and Nationality Act of 1965 welcomed people from around the world, especially those in difficult circumstances of poverty and war, the US Catholic Church also responded by welcoming these differing groups as part of their overall worship community. This recognition does not suggest that liturgical gatherings among differing languages, cultures, and peoples did not exist in various pockets of society throughout the United States prior to 1965. Rather, it signifies the recognition and inclusion of immigrants such as Catholics of Asian descent into US ecclesial structures.

By building on the momentum of the civil rights movement, students of Asian descent initiated a movement to empower themselves. By creating a new name, different from the labels given them during the discriminatory immigration period, these students identified themselves as Asian Americans. This political and social development also allowed within the church the ability to identify and nurture differing cultural groups from Asia. For example, the emergence of Korean American Catholics required both a social and religious development.

Korean American Catholics experienced a pivotal moment in 1966 when the Archdiocese of San Francisco acknowledged the growing commitment of Korean immigrants in their neighborhoods by establishing the first officially recognized Korean American Catholic community at St. Michael's. Although several communities existed across the United States prior to this declaration, the official sanctioning by a diocese meant that Korean Americans were now officially part of the US religious landscape. This milestone of being officially recognized is important today, because it is truly the "starting point" for Catholics of Korean descent. In other words, the ability to create an identity by reflecting on what it means to be Korean American Catholics would not have been possible without the cultural, social, and religious space afforded by the developments discussed above.

In 2016, Korean American Catholics will celebrate fifty years of their established cultural and religious heritage in the United States. This golden jubilee is also a culmination of the cultural and religious experience stemming from the emergence of the Catholic faith on the Korean Peninsula over a century ago and in this country after the Immigration and Nationality Act of 1965 and the Second Vatican Council. Cultural and religious celebrations revolving around the 1965 events in the church and the world demonstrate the relationship between the two that *Gaudium et Spes* supported but could not always envision.

Conclusion

After WWII, the world was torn in two as Cold War tensions reached new heights. The threat of communism began appearing all around the world and even near US shores as the Cuban Missile Crisis made the possibility of nuclear war not only real but also very close to home. In reaction to these threats, the United States felt the need to counteract the spread of communism by directly and indirectly engaging in regional conflicts across the globe. With a similar attitude, the Catholic Church also saw communism threatening faith practices of local communities. Therefore, Catholics in the United States had a double sense of duty to protect others from communist threat. The hierarchy as well as the laity opened the doors of their churches, neighborhoods, and even their own homes in welcoming those caught in the middle of the Cold War conflict. The hospitality shown during these times in the resettlement process reflected a sense of pride as both Catholics and Americans. Places like the Midwest where immigrants would otherwise have felt isolated became home and a new start to their lives because of the welcoming spirit of this country. The initial experience after legislative changes to immigration and the openness of the church to the world created a social and religious order like no other time in the history of this country. In addition to what was happening outside the country with the tensions of the Cold War, momentum from the civil rights movement provided new immigrants a sense of their destiny as well. The whirlwind of political and social developments was not fully understood, even by the people being directly affected; they allowed, however, both church and society the ability to identify and nurture differing cultural groups from around the world.

Chapter 6

Toward a Deeper Understanding of Biblical Promise

The Vietnamese American Catholic Experience

The sudden emergence of Vietnamese and other Southeast Asians on the American scene was primarily the result of U.S. military involvement in Southeast Asia. . . . The development of the communist bloc dominated by the former Soviet Union, the communist takeover in China, the direct confrontation with Communist troops in the Korean War, and the threat of Communist "domino" effect prompted a U.S. foreign policy to "contain" communism, pushing Americans into Southeast Asia.[1]

Although the departure of Vietnamese from their homeland happened hastily in many cases and occurred mainly in the post-1965 immigration period, these Southeast Asians are also able to document their immigration history in three waves, even though the dates and reasons for departure are quite different than their counterparts from other parts of Asia. While most Asian immigrants have some trace of their people departing their homeland for places like the United States prior to 1965, the Vietnamese people had not emigrated to the United States in any sizeable numbers like other ethnic groups from Asia prior to the Vietnam War. Rather, their stages of immigration have all occurred after the 1965 immigration reform under the refugee provisions.

The first wave began at the end of the Vietnam War with the fall of Saigon in 1975 and lasted until 1977. Many of those who were able to escape during the chaotic extraction of the US presence in Vietnam were somehow associated with either the US campaign against communism, affiliated with the South Vietnamese government and military, or were educated professionals living in urban areas. After the evacuation in the first wave, the next wave emerged and was made up of those without government or military connections as well as those less educated or living in rural areas, many who fled the harsh conditions and threats of the communist regime. It was during this time that the Vietnamese people who fled in this manner became known as the "Boat People" as they became refugees stranded either in neighboring countries or floating aimlessly in open waters. The third wave continued the influx of such Vietnamese refugees as Amerasians (children of US servicemen and Vietnamese women) and political prisoners; this third wave, however, now also included the immigration of the Vietnamese people through diplomatic channels. In addition to the initial surge of refugees after the US withdrawal from the region, Vietnamese refugees continued to leave their homeland even when the anticipated ongoing persecutions from the north did not materialize.[2]

> Several factors account for the lengthy flow of refugees from Vietnam. First, political repression continued to make life difficult for those individuals who were detained at or released from reeducation camps as well as for their family members. Second, economic hardships, exacerbated by natural disasters and poor harvest in the years following the war, created a widespread sense of hopelessness. Third, incessant warfare with neighboring countries further drained Vietnam's resources for capital investment and development. These severely adversarial conditions, triggering the second and third exodus of Vietnamese "Boat People" in the late 1970s and early 1980s, continued to send thousands of refugees off on the rugged journey to a better life.[3]

Perhaps just as bad, or even more brutal, than the war itself, was the voyage at sea, as practically everyone fleeing on these flotillas encountered not only the natural dangers of the open waters but also pirates who constantly harassed the helpless refugees. Due to the circumstances facing their departures, escape from their country could not be easily planned out and it took numerous attempts before fleeing Vietnam was even possible. Feeling like a breathing corpse, one escapee reminisced, "For nearly four years I tried just about every possible escape route from South Vietnam and failed. There were times I was even cheated by friends and relatives. Of course I kept my mouth shut: trying to escape was a serious crime, and if caught I could have been jailed for five years."[4] The uncertain elements of departure meant that minimal possessions were taken by the Boat People, especially in necessary resources such as food and water for the arduous unknown journey ahead. Basic necessities quickly became scarce commodities as the uncertain elements of being on open waters for an unknown length of time compounded the hardships of the exodus. One Vietnamese refugee recounted, "When even the smallest amount of rain fell, a mass of bodies crawled onto the plastic sheet, lapping up each droplet until our tongues bled."[5] Many shared similar experiences as they endured the same conditions of hardship throughout their journey.

> Our supplies of food and water ran out. I resorted to collecting rainwater by rigging up plastic sheets, but I couldn't harvest enough and my children became very seriously dehydrated. Raw, red sores were developing under my arms through using the oars—I had to eke out our fuel supply by rowing. My younger son begged me constantly for chicken rice and orange juice, but I could give him nothing but rainwater, and not enough of that. It was heartbreaking. I prayed hard for the horrible dream to end. I just wanted to wake up with all my children around me again. . . . I prayed and prayed and prayed.[6]

In addition to the harsh elements at sea, those floating aimlessly and not being immediately rescued, particularly women and children, also endured cruel attacks as they were stripped of their possessions as well as their dignity. Repeated incidents were common because of the multitude of pirates who persisted in violence and assaults on the most vulnerable Vietnamese.

We were violently stripped of our clothing as they searched for valuables. The men were then separated from the women and girls and told to remain on our boat while they forced the women onto theirs. . . . For five days they raped the girls and the women over and over and over. This all took place in front of a five-year-old boy and his three-year-old sister, who were taken on board along with their horrified mother. Eventually they released us, but three days later we were captured by another group of pirates. The fact that we now had nothing left for them to steal made them very angry, and they pulled out our gold teeth with pliers and beat us senseless afterwards.[7]

The images of thousands of refugees on the waters and in refugee camps in neighboring countries compelled the United States to adopt legislation to take measures regarding accountability for the devastation caused in Southeast Asia and to bring some relief to the chaotic aftermath of the void created by the withdrawal of US military presence.

The Refugee Act of 1980 became the most comprehensive piece of refugee legislation in U.S. history. In place of the "seventh preference category" established in 1965, which admitted refugees as part of the total number of immigrants allowed into the United States, the Refugee Act provided for an annual number of admissions for refugees, which was designated independent of the number of immigrants admitted and was to be established each year by the President in consultation with Congress. This legislative Act, then, became a policy of refugee resettlement, reflecting a continuing process, rather than a mere reaction to specific emergency events. . . . The Orderly Departure Program (ODP) was created in late May 1979 as an agreement between the United Nations High Commission for Refugees and the Hanoi government as a tentative solution to worldwide attention attracted by the Boat People.[8]

It should be noted that within these waves of immigration to the United States there has also been an ongoing movement of the Vietnamese people within this country. Whereas other Asian immigrants chose their destination cities because of their relational ties with the people already living there or their dream of starting over in a particular locale, Vietnamese immigrants were scattered throughout the country due to the strategies of relief organizations for refugee resettlement. Thus, these organizations dispersed the Vietnamese immigrants throughout the Midwest, where the influx of immigrants would not overburden the local population and even had local churches welcome the new arrivals to the country. During this period of resettlement, especially during the 1970s with the fall of Saigon, Christians in this country felt it was their duty to welcome the Vietnamese people, since they represented American presence in the world during the struggles against communism in the Cold War. At times, they seemed to adopt a kind of schizophrenic mentality, since Americans had embraced an antiwar attitude as the Vietnam War continued to escalate.

> This was only prevention, not eradication, of communism. However, most American people did not have enough political knowledge to understand this fact. Therefore, many young American students and citizens participated in the so-called anti-war demonstrations. . . . Others thought naively that their government was performing a futile humanitarian task for a far-away country, because people of that country did not have the sense of responsibility.[9]

This changing attitude, from their God-given calling to stop communism to now one of fatigue from their futile efforts, however, did not dampen their duty of receiving refugees with the collapse of South Vietnam. Relief organizations, churches, and individuals opened their hearts and homes to those caught in the conflict. In her book, *Autumn*, Mai Phuong tells of a typical initial encounter of Vietnamese refugees in their new surrounding after a long flight:

> "Your church is coming to meet your family." "My church?" "Yes. The church which is sponsoring you. They're over there." Looking ahead, Van saw a crowd of around thirty Americans waving at her. She was shocked. She never expected to be welcomed like that. . . . Now a group coming here at ten o'clock at night to meet

her family whom they never saw before, except a picture she sent them through the charity organization.[10]

The hospitality and care given to the Vietnamese people was greatly appreciated; the separation of the newly arrived to various regions where no other minorities existed, however, would have been difficult for any newcomer. While some Vietnamese immigrants settled in these outlying areas, most once again migrated to other regions of the country, settling in areas that not only resembled their homeland but also with other refugees seeking resettlement with one another. The familiarity of place and people was clearly evident in the resettlement of the Vietnamese people, as they not only accepted the local hospitality of both church and society, but sought to create a place of home and worship that resonated with their warm thoughts of their homeland along with the traumatic departure with one another.

Unlike other immigrants from Asia, the Vietnamese people did not necessarily benefit in the same manner from the 1965 Hart-Celler Act as those with a longer history of immigration to the United States. Prior to the Vietnam War, the Vietnamese American population was considered nonexistent because of the minute numbers found scattered across the country. The increase of Vietnamese Americans resulting from US withdrawal from that region and the country's ongoing instability eventually led to intense waves of departure. The massive exodus on water revealed the desperation of the situation and the willingness to sacrifice everything for any future possibilities. Therefore, the 1965 immigration legislation did not impact the Vietnamese immigrants in the same manner as those immigrants who came to the United States seeking better economic opportunities. The political situation after the fall of Saigon, however, initiated an exodus that took on similar patterns in a shorter and more accelerated time frame. Even though the Vietnamese immigration journey was spurred by different factors than Korean and Filipino immigration, they still trace their immigration history in three waves concurrent with the Immigration and Naturalization Act of 1965.

The Boat People's Prayer of Promise

The tragedy of people having to flee their homeland on any floating apparatus that would carry them away on open waters from the dangers of an oppressive regime is one that is quite common and shared among Vietnamese Americans who made the perilous journey and lived to tell about it. These shared experiences of escape by the Boat People have, however, not been captured in a way for those outside the Vietnamese American communities, nor the next generation, to truly comprehend and appreciate. Within the brutal context of the Boat People's plight, a spiritual dimension emerges, the goodness of humanity God has placed in us which no desperate situation can extinguish. A spirituality of hope that cannot be dampened by either human brutality or the devastating natural conditions of the sea is recounted time and again. There was nothing out there that could quench their spirits as revealed in the cry of the people. "By some miracle, we managed to hang on. To what, I don't know, but I prayed so hard I knew there was no way Jesus couldn't hear my prayers."[11]

Time after time, these prayers echoed through the watery landscape as the cruel conditions of being adrift did not wane. "As I stood at the edge of the boat, he held a gun to my head and told me to jump. And as I tethered on the brink of death, I knew my time had finally come. There would be no more running. No more lurking after dark. No more camouflaging myself. . . . [Somehow] Jesus had saved me."[12] The will to survive along with the miraculous moments of having their lives spared propelled Vietnamese refugees to continue on their quest, not only to freedom but also something even greater—being called forth by God's providential care.

> I thought it was some sort of statue of liberty, but a young boy shouted "Oil platform!" As we approached it, a ship appeared, but then passed the boat slowly. We called for help, but it was gone. Hastily I painted a sign in red paint on a piece of board: "SOS! You and God save us" [after being rescued and fed]. . . . The sky was blue, the sea was calm and a few dolphins were jumping up and playing alongside the ship. I suddenly felt very happy and said, "This is quite heavenly, isn't it."[13]

In hearing these stories of faith, especially vocation stories of priests just in my own diocese, a new appreciation for their dramatic departure surfaces not only as a historic reality but also, and more importantly, as a continuation of God's migrant people departing from their homeland—oftentimes under the harshest and cruelest of conditions. Often stories are told about how families fleeing on these boats offered prayers to God and included a promise—the successful escape from danger to another world of safety in exchange for the nurturing of their sons to the priesthood. This promise to have their children follow in the ways of God by service to God's people in the Catholic Church reflects a certain level of desperation. It is not, however, uncommon for people to call on their faith in the most difficult or crucial hour of their lives. It is also not uncommon for those in these types of situations to undergo a type of *metanoia* or conversion that is fulfilled in their offspring, a common theme seen in biblical motifs. This also helps explain the reason many leave their homelands and live as migrants for the fulfillment of their dreams in the next generation. What is even more amazing is how this dire situation where the prayer of promise is often offered up by parents transforms and even evangelizes those around.

Rather than have his parent offer a prayer of promise to the priesthood, one Vietnamese American priest took it upon himself to dedicate his own life to the priestly vocation if he survived the journey of the Boat People. At a critical moment when it was not just his own life that depended on these spiritual acts, Vincent Pham decided to make the promise to follow a priestly vocation as an offering for everyone floating together into the unknown.

> When my five brothers and I were young, my parents desired that at least one of us would one day become a priest, but their dream was shattered when the Communist government took over the country in 1975. It did not take this regime long to oppress people as they closed all Catholic institutions, except churches. Throughout the entire country, Catholics were not free to practice their faith. The new government endlessly issued many restrictions to control people's lives and local officers heartlessly enforced these new regulations. Seeing this daily oppression, without any

glimmer of hope for a better future, my parents decided to arrange for us to escape the country one by one. My journey was quite an ordeal since I was only 16 years old. In 1984, we escaped in a small boat with 51 others. The journey was an entire week, and it was a journey through hell from the very start. As soon as our boat took off, we were chased and shot by coastguards. Fortunately, we outran them and felt that God had saved us. We were beaten up by storms and robbed three times by pirates as we floated aimlessly on the ocean. It was during this time, I started praying for my death. I said many other prayers as well including a promise to give my entire life to God if we were saved from this ordeal. We were very tired and weak at this point, and only through a miracle did a merchant ship rescue us by hauling us ashore. We were saved. We eventually settled in California and I lived like any other teenager. It wasn't until my senior year when I was applying to several colleges that I remembered the prayer that I had cried out upon my escape. In the hopes of honoring God's providence at that moment of my life, I turned in my final application to St. John's Seminary. In 1997, I was ordained priest for the Diocese of Orange and ever since, served with a profound gratitude to God.[14]

Being compelled by their parents' spirituality, many young people made similar acts of faith, not only in moments of desperation, but also by the grace afforded them through the community's support. This support continued in both directions as the person making the promise to live a priestly life did so on behalf of those around him. The willingness to follow a priestly way of life was not an isolated decision but one that arose from the people's support for the person as well. Thus, the physical nurturing of the Boat People during their most difficult moments illustrates the spiritual reality of how mutually interdependent is the struggle for life.

Stories also abound about those who were not even Catholic at the time of departure and without any personal encounter with God other than maybe a Catholic education, who committed themselves in the prayer of promise similar to the one they heard from those around them making such commitments in the boat. The absence of catechism, spiritual guides, and other foundational aspects of the Catholic faith we take for granted so often illustrates once again the communal dimension of our faith journey. Through faith—revealed in prayers of promise along with the will for individual and communal survival—afforded young men and women the opening they needed in life to plead out to God for mercy. This way of evangelization is not as uncommon as one would imagine. The individualistic attitude that pervades our current society makes it difficult for us to imagine how commitments of this nature can be fulfilled, let alone be truly authentic. Yet salvation history is full of those coming to the faith through the faith of another. We see this in the encounters with Jesus, either through brother inviting brother, in the case of Andrew with Simon Peter, or on behalf of another, as with the centurion soldier; within these few examples we can see that faith is not a singular, individualistic act but is always witnessed in a communal setting.

Therefore, the promise of the Boat People to live a religious calling in life goes beyond just these examples of parents promising their child, young people making the promise themselves, and those coming to the faith and making the promise to follow God through the indirect evangelization of those around. These prayers of promise were historic moments of salvation history as many Vietnamese were able to flee their war-torn country but also helped in the settlement of the Vietnamese people in other countries. In the United States alone, there are over eight hundred Vietnamese American priests and several seminarians who continue to follow the path of those who went before them, even as the mass exodus from Vietnam, while still remembered may be becoming a more distant memory. The time removed from the actual experience raises two issues that need to be addressed not only by Vietnamese American communities but also by society in general as we look to pass on the faith to successive generations.

> U.S.-born Vietnamese children and those who arrived in the United States as infants have no clear personal memory of life in Vietnam, of the flight from the ancestral land, or of life in refugee camps. But they are still deeply affected by family histories and quasi-mythical accounts of life in the host country. Older generations pass on stories of the struggle to reach the new country.

> Even when the children dismiss these stories as remnants of a
> bygone era, the trials of the parents continue to influence their
> understanding of family history.[15]

The first is to not romanticize the tragedy of being forced out
of one's homeland. In addition, we must not identify the flight of
the Boat People as the only source of any vocation in leading a life
dedicated to God. The romanticizing of such events often fails to
resonate with the next generation as their lives are concerned with a
totally different reality, even though their reality is fueled by previous events. Also, the romanticizing of a tragic exodus fixates us on
one solution, rationale, mind-set, and development of people and
can at times begin to marginalize those who should be included
but feel alienated because they lack cultural or historical familiarity.

This brings us to the second issue of why we cannot romanticize
an awful tragedy for the sake of the second-generation Vietnamese
Americans who have no direct ties with the immigration exodus of
either the first or second wave after the fall of Saigon. In addition
to the context of the next generation now emerging within a totally
different reality than their parents, there is ongoing immigration of
the Vietnamese people to the United States in a third wave which
does not involve such drastic measures as seen in the first two
waves. Those in the third wave are now coming to the United States
as either immigrants or transnationals through proper immigration
channels, and even with the experience of the destruction during
and in the rebuilding of the country after the war, their outlook can
be quite different. Therefore, the continuation of the Vietnamese
American faith journey means honoring the efforts and dedication
and sacrifice of the Boat People in both the departure and resettlement of the Vietnamese people in the United States. Today's reality,
however, calls for further reflection on those born here without a
direct memory of the departure from Vietnam and those who are
in the United States through normal immigration protocols.

> It has been said facetiously—but not without a grain of truth—that
> first-generation Vietnamese Americans are concerned about how
> to be American *Vietnamese* and describe themselves primarily as

Vietnamese; second-generation Vietnamese Americans strive to be Vietnamese *American* and see themselves primarily as Americans; and third-generation Vietnamese Americans recognize that they are *both* American *and* Vietnamese and are deeply ambivalent about their primary identity. Needless to say, all three kinds of Vietnamese Americans have their own problems and challenges, a fact that it is wise to remember as we seek to understand them.[16]

The Biblical Understanding of Promise

From the illustration of the Boat People and other instances of pleading in moments of desperation, we sometimes fall into the trap of thinking of these moments as instinctual and not authentic moments of faith. The prime example of liberation, however, comes to us in the exodus event in the Old Testament. Prior to leaving their life of slavery and even afterward as free people, God's patience with the Israelites is repeatedly shown by an unbroken covenant made generations before. In fact, the act of liberation on God's part is spurred by the people's cry, a cry in desperate times.

> But the LORD said: I have witnessed the affliction of my people in Egypt and have heard their cry against their taskmasters, so I know well what they are suffering. Therefore I have come down to rescue them from the power of the Egyptians and lead them up from that land into a good and spacious land, a land flowing with milk and honey. . . . Now indeed the outcry of the Israelites has reached me, and I have seen how the Egyptians are oppressing them. Now, go! I am sending you to Pharaoh to bring my people, the Israelites, out of Egypt. (Exod 3:7-10)

Because of the prayers of the people in captivity in Egypt or on a boat off the coast of Vietnam, God hears the cry of the people and does not stand by but rather renews the covenant of old through the act of liberation. It is true that God is always the initiator of freedom—after all, God is the author of life; nonetheless, it is the cry of the people that triggers the decisive action throughout salvation history. The crying out to God in desperate moments of our lives must also be seen as true acts of faith and trust. How can someone plead or even complain to God in moments of crisis, if that person does not believe their cry will be heard? Thus, the prayer that arises from a cry of complaint or in desperation is also a prayer revealing another aspect of a deepening relationship with God.

The liberative act of God occurs in specific moments in history but also has layers of meaning for generations to come in understanding how God responds to the cry of the people. In the exodus event, God frees the people from the land of Egypt, *Miztrayim* (מצרים). The Hebrew word for Egypt refers to an actual location as well as signifying boundaries, limitations, or any constrictions within our lives. Seen in its broader context, the act of liberation in the Old Testament can also be a foreshadowing of the Boat People's salvation as their departure is also a result of being bound up and restricted within their country in the aftermath of civil war and the ongoing threat of the communist regime. Life in Vietnam resembled that of the Egyptian captivity of the Israelites, and the people's cries of prayer during their departure are similar to the cries of the original chosen people.

The act of God hearing the cry of the people and initiating the process of liberation through Moses reaches unprecedented heights in the Passover where the Israelites were protected from death prior to their exodus out of slavery as God's reminder to the people of a promise made long ago. The Passover illustrates the promise of God in a specific moment when God's own are in dire straits. At this moment of captivity, it is not the people of faith that make a promise to God but, rather, it is God who promises to spare his own with the blood of the lamb. The protection of the blood on the doorpost of the people of God is also a valuable lesson for the Israelites—not only a lesson to cry out for assistance but also concurrent with this pleading, a lesson that is quite fitting for God to remember and renew a covenant of old. As the Israelites move into the desert and are surrounded by new challenges living on their own, they once again encounter a situation of being reminded of God's covenant with them and this time the promise becomes solidified in legal codification. The event at Mount Sinai and the giving of the Ten Commandments reveal once again a promise being renewed by God and fulfilled in the people's call to enter the Promised Land.

During the exodus, the uncertainty of the struggle for life is staged on the waters of chaos. Turmoil exists not only because of the winds and waves that buffet those around it but also because the waters are in God's domain and humanity has no control over them. We see similar themes developed from the very beginning when the Spirit hovered over the waters of chaos, bringing order to creation in Genesis. Also, in the Old Testament, the overwhelming waters of heaven and earth consume the world in destruction during the time of Noah. In the New Testament, Jesus walks on water as a theophany and calms the waves when awoken by those around him who were scared. Therefore, the open waters in the Hebrew mind-set are truly the realm of God and acts surrounding them constitute a miracle since they are strictly God's doing. Through the waters, creation is brought to order and becomes the backdrop for God's ultimate act for humanity—salvation. Liberation of God's people in the exodus event is a process beginning with the departure from captivity in the land of Egypt. The liberative act, however, reaches a culmination in the Red Sea as God's chosen pass safely through the divided waters while the Egyptian pursuers are eradicated once and for all.

In the case of the Vietnamese Boat People, many parallels can be made between the exodus event and their own plight. Through these connections, God's providence in leading the people to salvation can also be witnessed. The Vietnamese Boat People wander helplessly on the open waters since they, too, have no control over the ocean. The pursuers during the Vietnamese escape are pirates who oppress the vulnerable just as the Egyptians did over a thousand years before the time of Christ. Just as with the liberative act of salvation occurring on the waters for the Israelites, the Vietnamese Boat People experience a similar type of liberation that leads to salvation in every aspect of their lives. The liberative act is not just being able to overcome or control the elements at sea; the liberation of God's people comes in the form of a rescue in a boat. From Noah, to Moses, and now to the Vietnamese people, the symbol of being saved in the confines of a water vessel on the waters is part of the narrative of salvation history.

Tebah (תֵּבָה) is the Hebrew term associated with salvation. *Tebah* is the ark that Noah was commanded to build in preparation for the coming flood. Through the *tebah*, Noah, his family, and all living creatures were able to survive the destructive waters. *Tebah* is also the Hebrew word for the basket that Moses floated down the river in when he was only a baby. In order to survive, his mother placed the infant in a *tebah* so that he could be discovered by the Egyptians and given an opportunity at life. Thus, the Vietnamese people floating haphazardly on the open waters was a great tragedy in the midst of other tragedies on shore. In the midst of such dangers, however, God's liberative act is realized through a wooden vessel once again. It is the wandering away from the homeland on a wooden boat that gave life to the Vietnamese people even after enduring the cruel natural elements of the sea and the atrocities committed by other human beings. In addition, I am certain there must have been those who questioned their decision to leave in this manner, especially when difficult conditions were suffered time and time again. These people probably wished they had never started this arduous journey and quickly forgot the difficulties of remaining in Vietnam, not unlike the Israelites who grumbled in their wandering of the desert for forty years. God's faithfulness, however, especially in hearing the cry of God's people in these types of scenarios, never fails. Not only does God allow the people to find relief in their journey, many similarities can be found in our own journeying to help us identify God's providence, liberation, and salvation.

Another similarity between the Israelites in their journey to the Promised Land and the Vietnamese Boat People in their quest to reach safer shores, especially the United States, is found in historical memory. The difficulties of escape from Vietnam are not always relayed to others in such striking detail but more in commonalities that people shared in such an arduous journey. Even so, the retelling of such stories lifts ordinary men, women, and children who left under such difficult conditions into becoming "heroes" for generations to come. In a similar fashion, the Israelites who journeyed out of slavery into freedom were remembered time and time again for their heroism, even when this was not their intention. The moving forward of their own lives, however, whether by choice or by force, allowed future generations to give thanks for their efforts in creating a new reality for the present generation. Stories about the *tebah* are stories about the faith voyage of unsung heroes who braved troubled waters.

Therefore, a promise in difficult times is not uncharacteristic of the faith journey or seen as an act of desperation. Often our own ideals of commitment devalue promises made when no other solutions are available. In addition, our own inability to keep these promises further undermines the importance of promises made in these crucial moments. Examples throughout salvation history reveal that these promises are constantly made, broken, and renewed. Eventually, the repetition of the limitations of humanity humbles us into true conversion where an understanding of God's love is witnessed in the covenant made so long ago. Without these promises in challenging moments of our lives, especially when everything is at risk (including life itself) for ourselves as well as those around us, the opportunities of bettering relationships and deepening our understanding of God's covenant with us remains distant. Only in our promises, regardless of our limited abilities of faithfulness, do God's covenant and promises made throughout history become familiar and truly our own today as well.

Our Lady of La Vang

An interesting process of resettlement arising from the Vietnamese immigration to the United States is found in the religious development of the people in diaspora, in particular, the image of Our Lady of La Vang. The historical telling of the apparition in Vietnam was done through oral transmission beginning in 1798 when Catholics were being persecuted. During their hiding in the forest, Mary appeared as one of their own both in appearance and in dress. Her title as the Lady of La Vang is quite fitting for those she appeared to, since within her name the plight of Catholics at that time is captured, as La Vang can either mean, "to cry out" or "leaves of the tree or herbal seed."

> She appeared as a beautiful lady wearing a dress and long cape, holding a baby and accompanied by two angels. She heard their

cry for help and her message was that she would always help them in time of need. The Virgin Mother gave the people solace and instructed them to boil the la' vang leaves for use as a medicine. She also said that from that day on, all who come to this place would have their prayers heard and answered.[17]

Given the fact that Catholics were in hiding in the forest and had many moments of needing to cry out during the persecution, the title is quite fitting, since La Vang encapsulates the struggles of the faithful she watches over. In fact, the geographic connections of the La Vang apparition as well as similarities to another Vietnamese goddess, Kwan Yin, allowed for an even greater embracing of this apparition. Therefore, the historical accuracy of this oral tradition and whether it should be counted as one of the authentic apparitions within the church is still being debated, even though the faithful have moved well past these discussions, as revealed by their unfettered devotion to their cultural Madonna.

> A few points of distinction about the La Vang apparitions are that unlike the apparitions in Europe, especially at Lourdes and Fatima which were institutionally approved, Mary's message was of apocalyptic divine punishment, in Vietnam it was of protection and well-being. Mary's [care of God's children] creates the image of a divine mercy that speaks so powerfully to Vietnamese Catholics who have been persecuted since missionary times.[18]

As the faithful have moved forward in their devotional life to La Vang, their image of Our Lady has evolved with the immigration process. The image presented at the two hundredth anniversary of Our Lady of La Vang is culturally more accurate than possibly at any other time in Vietnamese Catholic history. Initially, through the French Catholic influence in Vietnam, La Vang was presented as Our Lady of Victory inside the church dedicated to the apparition in 1900. Therefore, a very European-looking image of Mary continued within this Vietnamese Marian devotion. This foreign influence had its benefits as well as disadvantages. By portraying the Vietnamese apparition as a familiar Madonna, it was easier for the European missionaries to accept the appearance as a genuine occurrence of the faith. The European image, however, obscured what was clearly a distinct Vietnamese apparition based on location, context, and dress, not only during the dedication of the church for the Blessed Mother, but also for generations to come. Only centuries later would a culturally sensitive and culturally correct image of La Vang appear, restoring the deeper Marian significance to the Vietnamese people.

> The first attempt to indigenize or Vietnamize Our Lady of La Vang was through the efforts of Vietnamese Catholics living in Southern California. . . . In 1994, Vietnamese American Catholics in Orange County, California constructed their version of Mary first named Our Lady of Vietnam. Van Nhan, a Vietnamese artist and sculptor, created the statue. They did not initially call her Our Lady of La Vang but Our Lady of Vietnam. Visiting priests from the Diocese of Hue, Vietnam invited Van Nhan to create a new statue of Our Lady of La Vang molded on the Our Lady of Vietnam that he had previously sculpted. Our Lady of Vietnam now becomes Our Lady of La Vang. This change for the Vietnamese in diaspora is significant as she is shifted from a national symbol to a very Catholic [universally applicable] one, placing her in a unique historical position.[19]

Remarkable lessons can be gleaned from the contributions of the people in diaspora, especially to their homeland. The Vietnamese Marian experience is an example *par excellence* of the responsibility and task of the local communities to contribute not only to those surrounding them in resettlement but also back to the homeland that gave them their initial life. The ability of the Vietnamese in the United States to conceive of a cultural image of Our Lady of La Vang and have it represent the national image back home is nothing short of amazing in itself. Often, those living abroad focus on the economic in giving back to their homeland; they rarely see their spiritual developments as a vital contribution for the growth of those back home. At best, the adjustment in the church for immigrants are difficult enough and frequently hinder any attention that can be given to culturally based developments impacting their homelands. Even with these obstacles as immigrants in a foreign society, however, the task of further reflecting on the cultural aspects of the faith can be heightened and from their situation, a more advantageous view of the situation can sometimes be found, as in the case of culturally restoring Our Lady of La Vang.

The cultural identification of the faith, even for those living in the United States, is a necessary endeavor in order to create a suitable sacred space of their own. Within this creation, others in the United States and those back home are then invited in as well. Without such developments, there are no invitations extended; without this aspect of hospitality, a community becomes insular and never truly part of the wider church through their connection with the local parish communities, diocesan structures, and eventually the universal aspect of the faith. Many communities simply construct independent buildings as a way of separating their worship space from those around them. These independent structures, however, are not truly cultural worship spaces needed to benefit the local communities in their connection with the wider church. Separate churches foster ghetto-like communities which do not allow these communities to see the importance of their gatherings and truly value the contributions they are able to make to others. Instead, the creation of ethnic faith communities is important not only for those immediately impacted but also for the entire Catholic Church, as their reflections impact not only their own but also the entire church's liturgical celebration.

Thus, the "Vietnamizing" or cultural reappropriation of La Vang from a European version to an image that resonates with the people of the local village is truly a gift from the Vietnamese people in diaspora. By making Mary our own, a renewal or discovery for the first time emerges both in our spiritual as well as our cultural identities. In doing so, a profound reason for departure from the homeland can be discovered, as one's contribution gives confidence to live and pray in an entirely different set of circumstances. The Vietnamese American Catholic gift in the image of Our Lady of La Vang has immense implications for all Vietnamese Americans, regardless of religious affiliation. The reason for this is that confidence, the pride of an entire people, is lifted by witnessing a contribution of this magnitude.

Perhaps only those living in diaspora are able to have a unique perspective of their own cultural and spiritual lives because they cannot take for granted what is simply encountered back home. When this discovery betters oneself, one's local community, one's home country, and even the entire church, then it becomes an important reminder of the overall task of Christianity, a task to go and make disciples. For the early church, the making of disciples was not on the terms of the evangelizers but according to the context of those being converted as at "the Council of Jerusalem to open the church to the Gentiles on the Gentile's terms."[20] The encounters found in the expansion of our lives becomes the fundamental context in renewing our spiritual and cultural perspective, allowing us to align ourselves better with God's reign.

Conclusion

In his book on Vietnamese American Catholics, Peter Phan includes a Vietnamese way of doing theology.[21] The steps he accounts for the Vietnamese people must take in the context of the Vietnamese Americans for any theological reflection to occur. Included in this reflection are the events of departure and resettlement as well as folkloric myths from the homeland, which together help form the consciousness of the Vietnamese American people. From this understanding of who the Vietnamese American people are, Christian sources (Scripture and tradition) can then be applied to specific situations of the Vietnamese American experience to give greater light to what it means to be Catholics in this specific ethnic faith group. Finally, reflection must lead to some form of concrete activity in society resembling Jesus' outreach to those who are often neglected by their own. Thus, Phan writes, "A Vietnamese theology must necessarily be both active contemplation and contemplative action. And this critical practice will in turn bring new materials and resources to the theological mill to generate another cycle of critical analysis and interpretation and praxis."[22]

Phan's thoughts on how to do a distinct theology is not only applicable to Vietnamese American Catholics but it is also a necessary reflection for all groups to properly understand their existence and purpose in God's plan of salvation. The beginning stages of theological reflection start with the people being reflected on. Often our reflections begin during a certain plight, sometimes at a deepest hour of need. Our minds remember these events to the point that our bodies also react to such memories and therefore are never truly lost. Memories, however, also need to be recalled in some fashion that gives them continuity and meaning and not simply in the manner of collecting data. For Vietnamese Americans, the promises of the Boat People are gateways for the faithful to stay connected to the events of salvation history of old as well as of those in today's reality.

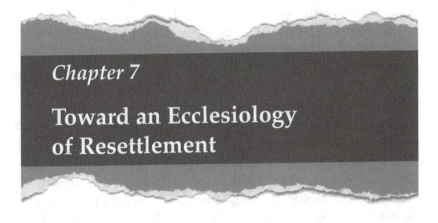

Chapter 7

Toward an Ecclesiology of Resettlement

The Filipino American Catholic Experience

Immigration to the United States by the people of the Philippines has existed since the eighteenth century. Over two-and-a-half centuries of immigration based on economic and educational reasons have been categorized into four stages: 1763–1906, 1906–1934, 1945–1965, and 1965 to the present.

> Economic hardship, political repression, and close ties with the United States motivated continued emigration from the Philippines after the country gained independence. The United States' bases in the Philippines were the former's principal presence in the Pacific during the Cold War, guaranteeing continued close ties between Filipinos and Americans. The United States government was the second-largest employer of Filipinos after the Philippines government, with 68,000 Filipinos on the U.S. payroll. By 1970, there were more Filipinos in the U.S. Navy than in the Philippines Navy, and between 1946 and 1965, half of all immigrants from the Philippines were wives of U.S. servicemen. After nationality quotas were removed from U.S. immigration law in 1965, women from the Philippines immigrated in larger numbers, many to fill demand in the care sector: in 2011, 18 percent of Filipino immigrant women worked as registered nurses, while many other worked in child and elder care.[1]

Even with their distinct immigration experience to the United States, several commonalities with other immigrants from Asia seem to appear during earlier years and more so after the Second World War. The bulk of the shared immigration experience between differing groups, however, begins post-1965 in the latest wave of Filipino migration to the United States. Since the majority of the shared history of immigration for non-European immigrants is a result of the 1965 immigration revisions, this period is what is pertinent to our examination of the emergence of the complexity of the local church today.

Filipinos who came to the United States after the Second Vatican Council desired to create a cultural-religious space for themselves like any other immigrants now that the council had opened the church to the recognition, preservation, and incorporation of other cultures into existing church structures. The creation of a sacred space that allows people to maintain their cultural identity in a universal religious experience is a valid concern for all immigrant groups. Both religious as well as secular space affords protection, comfort, and opportunities for growth for those departing and trying to settle into a new home. Unlike other Asians, the challenge for Filipino immigrants in creating their own space in terms of a church building, community center, or some sort of distinguishing space that culturally represented their own was attributed to linguistic compatibility. In most other cases, language becomes the identifying marker to whether an ethnic group needs their own worship space to incorporate their cultural differences in prayer. Because of linguistic barriers, many instinctively support the creation of at least an alternative Mass, prayers, and sacred space to accommodate the cultural dissimilarities associated with linguistic differences. Therefore many Catholic groups, such as those of Vietnamese or Korean descent, are continuing to establish their own ethnic faith communities along with the necessary structures to support their sacramental, social, and cultural realities.

The challenge for Filipino American Catholics was the presentation of their own ethnic group as culturally different, even though a similar language was shared with the English speaking communities. Without a linguistic difference that afforded other ethnic groups their own cultural and religious space, Filipino American Catholics were faced with the challenge of presenting their own cultural distinction, a challenge few other post-1965 immigrants were faced with. What Filipino American Catholics encountered with the US Church is similar to the challenges that African American Catholics had to overcome and are still grappling with—the issue of how to transmit a cultural difference to those around them even if one speaks the same language. For African American Catholics, the challenge was to demonstrate to other Catholics in this country that the English language was expressed and received in a profoundly different manner for black Catholics. The historical realities of slavery, racism, and discrimination that form the backdrop of black consciousness give significantly different values and meanings to the English language by not only what is said but also by whom it is said. Thus, African Americans desire to worship within the confines of a language and expression befitting their use of the English language by those who are well versed in the cultural and generational complexity of this particular faith community. Trying to relay this reality when one shares the same birthplace, citizenship, and language is difficult, but overcoming this challenge has given black Catholics some space for them to navigate and embrace the faith as their own, as evident by the National Black Catholic Congress along with a national pastoral plan for black Catholics.

Filipino immigrants faced similar challenges if not greater ones when coming to the United States and desiring to create their own space. It is often thought that Filipino Catholics had no desire or need for the creation of their own personal worship space. The Filipino faith experience in diaspora countries other than the United States, however, has been a different one. Rather than blending in with the communities already in existence, Filipinos in other countries have expressed a desire for the creation of their own cultural worship space, much like other immigrants in the United States. One researcher in Italy found that although many Catholic immigrants seek assistance in resettlement from the local church, they do not have the same eagerness in coming together into the same worship space.[2] Clearly, the linguistic hurdle is evident in situations like these and thus, Filipino immigrants voice the need for their own cultural way of worship where English is not the primary language. The experience of these Filipino Catholics has been very different from their counterparts in the United States. Some valuable lessons can, however, be gleaned from their similarities and differences. Most importantly, immigrants, regardless of their linguistic familiarities, still desire a personal cultural worship that preserves the heritage of their homeland and also allows them to transcend the immediate environs of their new homeland.

Because Filipinos speak English, it was difficult for them to convince the leadership in the United States of their cultural distinctness and advocate for their own needs for a culturally oriented sacred space. Rather, they were guided to merge into the existing English-speaking communities since there were virtually no linguistic challenges in either case. Ignoring other cultural markers such as biological differences, dress, and other verbal and nonverbal expressions hindered Filipinos from addressing fully their cultural and spiritual needs. Any loss in cultural expressions of the faith was also a loss in contributing to the wider church. Certain cultural expressions of the faith, however, have been preserved in seasonal liturgical celebrations such as *Simbang Gabi* or *Fiesta ni Maria*. Unfortunately, the adaptation or preservation of these cultural expression into the life of the US church is not yet widely known.

The preservation of these devotional practices that incorporate their cultural heritage within a religious realm highlights the need for a distinct vernacular to capture the nuances of the people's prayer. Devotions are deeply rooted in cultural expressions and historic conditioning and cannot be maintained simply by the familiar language of the hearer. In reality, both the speaker and the hearer must have a common ground for such devotional practices to resonate. The prayers that emerge from these devotions capture a sense of Filipino identity that draws the hearts of those experiencing the religious moment in and makes them feel like they are at home, much like familiar sustenance we relate to as "comfort food." Thus the preservation of linguistic expressions, in addition to cultural spaces of worship, are vital in popular religiosity, the intimate spiritual practices that bring us closer to the universality of our faith.

A Unified Resilience

> Although more than eighty percent of Filipinos are Roman Catholic, this, along with a colonial country name, misleads non-Filipinos, including Filipinos themselves, to think that Philippine culture is very different from her neighboring countries, but this is not entirely so. The Philippines is very much like her neighboring countries in that the dominant religions in these countries (i.e., Buddhism, Christianity, Hinduism, Islam, etc.) are assimilated with a myriad of local animistic or traditional practices common throughout, producing a unique belief system.[3]

The Philippines consists of 7,107 islands that contribute to the diversity of the Filipino people. At the same time, the multitude of islands is the source of differences between the inhabitants of this country. In addition, this massive combination of different islands also creates a sense of independence illustrated by the different languages and customs possessed by different island natives. Certain languages such as Tagalog or English create some commonality because of the linguistic familiarity between the differing groups; however, distinguishing oneself into regional groups is still the norm. "Although the British are credited for introducing English in the Philippines in 1762, it was the American troops followed by the [1,100 teachers sent over to teach in the 'American' educational system] that taught the English reading and writing skills."[4] Even with the reinforcement of not only the English language but also a Western lifestyle, a common tongue did not bridge the cultural gaps between the differing island populations. Linguistic similarities have a definite advantage in facilitating the communication between different peoples; nevertheless, the unifying force for Filipinos was rather the Catholic faith. Sacramental worship of the one true God unites the many languages and diverse backgrounds of the Filipino people. This unity of faith does not disregard one's background but transcends the diverse settings from island to island into a *communio* of faith where the various customs are still valued and accepted. There is no doubt that the English language assisted in promoting a systematic way of communicating the Catholic way of life; the necessary component, however, was the visible spiritual reality provided by the Catholic Church.

Even the diversity of peoples stemming from the multitude of islands did not keep the Filipino people from quickly receiving one another as brothers and sisters. Reinforced by the biblical notions of hospitality, Filipinos became well adept at opening their homes and hearts to the people around them. Filipinos have been at home with each other as either the host receiving others or as guests making their temporary surroundings much like their own home. Hospitality is now so engrained in the Filipino mind-set that neither racial, gender, nor religious prescriptions override this cultural practice. The expectation of opening one's doors to others, along with the ability to adapt to many environments because of the welcome they received, have made Filipinos resilient in various situations, a quality that would become crucial in the immigration experience. This resilience in making their home wherever and with whomever is a great advantage of the Filipino people. In particular, this natural inclination to being hospitable and receiving hospitality allowed the immigrants to adjust to the existing local faith communities in the United States.

The Philippines is mostly an agrarian society outside its main metropolitan hub. Farmers are constantly at work in the fields to ensure a healthy crop for their families and the lives of those around them. This task becomes especially difficult when series of typhoons plague the islands, an average of twenty-eight annually wreaking havoc on the crops when reaching landfall. Farmers are consistently resowing their crops in the field, typhoon after typhoon, symbolizing both an immediate hope found in the yearly crops as well as an ongoing hope in their faith journey through the repetitive cycle of cultivation for the future. The repetitive action of maintaining one's crop season after season in these difficult conditions further represents the resiliency of the Filipino people. Not discouraged by natural disasters, Filipino farmers press forward in the hope of a bounty at harvest time. In addition, the spirit and attitude that emerges under these difficult situations is reflective of the Filipino people's trust in God. A major motivation is the notion that God will never abandon his people so that even nature's chaos cannot discourage the efforts of God's will for the people.

It would not suffice to speak about the resiliency of the Filipino people without mentioning their colonial encounters. Although many atrocities occurred during the foreign occupation of the Philippines, these encounters also reinforced the spirit of resiliency in the native people. Through their encounters with other cultures and peoples because of their strategic position for economic, military, and even religious purposes, the Filipino people had to continually adapt. As early as the seventh century, Filipinos encountered the Chinese people when trade relations were established with the Tang dynasty. Since then the economic ties with China would leave a cultural legacy as Chinese words, dress, customs and other foreign, but useful aspects were incorporated into the Filipino way of life. Other influences also emerged on Philippine soil following the Chinese trade route. Traces of the Muslim and Hindu encounter can also be found in the native language and social customs found on the various islands.

In the sixteenth century, with the arrival of the Spanish explorer Ferdinand Magellan, the Filipino political, social, and religious landscape would forever change. Originally under the auspices of New Spain, the Philippines would become a colony of the European power. With the Spanish presence came not only linguistic differences but also a religious practice in Catholicism. Any political matters included religious thought and any religious missionary movements required state intervention as well. Therefore, the conversion of souls of the Filipino people also included a social and political transformation. This colonial system would continue in varying degrees until the nineteenth century, when the Philippines came under the control of the United States at the end of the Spanish-American War with the Treaty of Paris in 1898.

US control in a colonial or imperialistic manner lasted until the Second World War when Japanese military forces occupied the country between 1942 and 1945. After the end of the war, the US preoccupation in rebuilding Europe left the Philippines to develop mostly on its own. The impact of the Cold War being felt in all parts of the world, however, made the Philippines a strategic military outpost for the United States in their push for containment of communism. US military presence lasted until 1992 when the Philippine senate voted to close down the naval base at Subic Bay. There have been many other foreign encounters over the history of the Philippines that have not been mentioned here, those which also have left an indelible cultural or religious mark on the Filipino people. This brief overview of the historic encounters with foreign powers, however, illustrates the impact, both negative and positive, on this island nation.

With each foreign presence, the Filipino people had to accommodate their way of life with the foreigners regardless of whether it was by force or by choice. This adaptive lifestyle has become a strength in dealing with others not only in the Philippines but also, perhaps more importantly, in the encounters outside the Philippines as Filipinos emigrate for better opportunities elsewhere. This ability to adjust to other environs and other peoples is not only evident in their social resettlement but has also been a helpful advantage in settling within the US Catholic Church given the cultural blinders encountered. Even though distinct places of worship did not materialize for the Filipino people in the United States, their physical, emotional, and spiritual resilience has allowed them to make the United States their spiritual and cultural home.

Saints on the Move

The Filipino saints are interesting case studies with similarities and differences with other saints who endured martyrdom especially in Asia. The ultimate sacrifice by dying for the faith is the overall common characteristic in Saints Lorenzo Ruiz and Pedro Calungsod with martyrs who have gone before and after them. What is unique about these two, nevertheless, is that the challenges to their faith did not happen in their home country. Rather than having to defend their beliefs in the Philippines, both Filipino saints were tested in their faith while abroad. Historically, those of different ethnicities living and dying for the faith in a foreign land were usually missionaries. For example, within the cluster of martyrs in Asia from places like Vietnam or Korea, several European missionaries are often scattered among the numbers because of mission activities in those parts of the world. Neither Ruiz nor Calungsod, however, were missionaries in the strict sense of the word, and even their departure from the Philippines included some questionable motives. Regardless, their ability to settle into their new environment and excel in their faith is what the church finds exemplary today.

Although upheld for the valor of faith they demonstrated in a foreign land, both these men model for the church a way of immigration and how to live one's life in resettlement. Lorenzo Ruiz fled his native land in the first half of the seventeenth century because of an incident involving the death of a Spaniard. Ruiz went into exile with Dominicans who gave him safe passage to Japan. Even before his arrival, a persecution of Christians was underway in Japan as the Tokugawa shogunate issued a decree banning the Catholic faith in 1614. Thus, hostility toward Catholics greeted Ruiz and his Dominican travelers upon their arrival in Japan in 1636. A year later, Ruiz, along with other Catholics who did not apostatize, found themselves gathered at Nagasaki where they were eventually martyred for the faith in 1637. Whether one believes the first Filipino saint to be accidental, finding himself in the midst of a situation that led to canonization, or if his faith convictions led to his death with the other fifteen martyrs who were canonized with him in 1987, Ruiz is still a model for both immigration and resettlement for the church.

Similarly, Pedro Calungsod left the Philippines after being selected to accompany missionaries to Guam due to his skills as both a sacristan and catechist in the second half of the seventeenth century. In evangelizing Chamorrans, especially through the sacramental process of infant baptism, some natives accused Calungsod and others of attempting to poison their people after some babies died shortly after their baptism. This accusation eventually led to the persecutions of Christians where Calungsod and others who were with him at their last infant baptism were martyred in 1672.

He and six others were canonized for their missionary efforts in 2012. Unlike Ruiz, who left in haste from a questionable situation, Calungsod's case is more appealing because of the nature of his departure from the Philippines. Both candidates, however, are good models of immigrants and the immigration process of re-settlement that need further reflection to deepen how immigrants should continue to carry out, even die, for their faith in diaspora.

Why are both Filipino saints models of immigration? Even though the lives of both these holy men took place many centu-ries ago, they typify the nature of departure for many immigrants regardless of region or time. Departure from one's homeland, especially in the post-1965 immigration period, is attributed to various reasons, oftentimes either for very common reasons such as the devastation left after regional conflicts or civil wars or for less common variables from countries of origination where no clear conflicts existed. In either case, the anticipated or unantici-pated causes for immigration are captured in the lives of Ruiz and Calungsod. In addition, the unexpected encounters in a foreign land because of one's cultural and religious heritage cannot be separated from the events that occurred in Japan or Guam. These events not only symbolize the trials and tribulations found in moments of resettlement but they also reveal the rewards for the faithful in both the living out of the faith and in the dying for something they truly believe in.

Small Base Communities of Faith

Smaller religious gatherings outside the eucharistic celebration, oftentimes in rural areas, were formed to provide accountability and support in the daily living out of the Catholic faith. Often as-sociated with Latin America, these base communities also thrived in parts of the Philippines known as basic Christian communities (BCC) even prior to Vatican II. Bishop Julio Labayen of the Philip-pines comments,

> If we are honest we have to admit that there does not yet exist in the church a means, outside of the BCCs, by which ordinary

Christians can attain equality and participate democratically in the life of the church. For this reason the BCCs concretize for the first time Vatican II's vision of a living church that is decentralized, open, respectful of the autonomy of the secular and the laity's competence, a servant church, but one with a clear and uncluttered view of what its task in the world is: evangelization of the whole of life—economic, political, social, cultural.[5]

These small cells form the *communio* model of church discussed by the council fathers and have become "as important for the life of the church as the decision made by the Council of Jerusalem to open the church to the Gentiles on the Gentiles' terms."[6] Rather than a hierarchical, pyramidal structure of the past, Vatican II's vision of the church was re-presenting church with its central system not in a linear fashion but as one of the many necessary cells that make up the Body of Christ that is in the world. Bishop Labayen reinforces this relationship with the world as realized in the BCCs:

> There is mutual convergence between the building of people's organizations and the Basic Christian Communities. The former is basically secular and the latter religious, but they share the same bias for equality and participation and they are for the poor. If the BCCs are the religious concretization of the vision of Vatican II, then true peoples' organization, are the secular concretization. They are two sides of the same coin.[7]

It is also this ability to form smaller, more intimate communities of faith as authentic expressions of the fullness of church that have contributed to the resettlement of Filipino Catholics in the United States. Filipino Catholics have settled into the landscape of the US Catholic Church much more easily than most post-1965 Catholic immigrants because of the lack of linguistic and communal hurdles. The ability to form intimate faith groups has allowed them to connect culturally and spiritually with one another in a foreign land while still being able to navigate the social and ecclesial landscape of the host country. In short, Filipino Catholics possess all the tools and skills necessary for resettlement in the United States because of their previous experiences of church as small faith communities within the wider church. Their experience as immigrants parallel this movement where their incorporation to the local parish communities has also allowed them to feel like part of the wider US Church, a part of the global religious community with their ongoing connections with the faith of their homeland, and also as members of the universal church with Catholics worldwide. While some immigrant groups have been able to associate with some levels of church life, whether strictly in their local community or as an extension of the church from their homeland, Filipino Catholics have navigated various levels of ecclesial life by embracing the fundamentals necessary for sustaining the faith in addition to greater measures necessary in maintaining the unity of faith within cultures.

Maternal Presence for Resettlement

Many factors, some listed in this chapter and some yet to be uncovered, allowed Filipino immigrants to resettle in the United States with greater ease than other Asian ethnic groups. In fact, the combination of these factors coming together in the immigration experience to the United States might be the greatest asset in the resettlement process. Rather than just relying on one historic encounter or distinct Filipino characteristic, the culmination of all their cultural and religious traits have allowed Filipino Catholics to blend in with the social and ecclesial fabric of the United States. While other ethnic faith groups may possess similar abilities or traits, the combination of these factors are unique to the Filipino people.

For example, Vietnamese Catholics have been evangelized by European missionaries as well. Not only did the French missionaries evangelize this region of Southeast Asia, they also developed written Vietnamese through a series of combinations of the Roman alphabet. Even with this outside influence, the Vietnamese people still have a greater hurdle in reaching the same degree of linguistic compatibility as their Filipino counterparts in the United States. The French linguistic influence was not as important a factor in their resettlement in the United States, while the Filipinos' ability to speak English or Spanish gave them a tremendous advantage in navigating their new home. The French missionaries' respect for the linguistic heritage of the Vietnamese people was evident by their creation of a completely unique Roman-style alphabet that complemented the existing spoken Vietnamese language.

Korean Catholics also share a history of being occupied by foreigners in their homeland or being caught in between warring neighbors desiring to expand their borders. The foreign presence in their country, however, has made them more isolated than open to others as a result of their experience of resistance and expulsion of foreign characteristics in an effort to purify their identity. Rather than building on the values and benefits from these painful moments, Koreans have rejected any disgraced moments by striving to excel at anything they engage in. In particular, the striving to overcome their painful struggles of the past have made them successful, not by employing the lessons learned from the past, but rather by using them strictly as motivation for success. The utilization of these moments to spur the Korean people forward in progress, however, has not opened them to other cultures in the same manner as Filipino society. Rather, Koreans have raised their own country, people, and even church above others instead of raising themselves with the people around them.

Therefore, Filipinos have much more significant and beneficial contact with foreigners in their own homeland and the culmination of these experiences over the years has been a great asset for the Filipino people at home and especially in their emigration abroad. Of particular interest for the resettlement in the United States is the matriarchal nature of the Filipino people and how this unique Asian feature bridges some of the cultural differences between the Philippines and the United States. Since other Asian countries are primarily patriarchal, they do not have the same experience of bridging the cultural divide as evident in the Filipino resettlement. Since Filipinas are heads of the household, they are also the ones more likely to marry outside of their culture in the United States than are their male counterparts. The result of these interracial marriages is the ability to bridge the Filipino world they derive from within the US reality they enter into, especially through marriage. In addition to keeping their Filipino identity as head of the household, they are also able to pull their spouses from a different culture into the Filipino reality through celebrations, customs, and food, to name a few things.

Similar to many Asian cultures, it is uncommon for Filipino males to marry someone from another country, while it is much easier for Filipino females to enter into such a relationship. Also, when other Asian females marry outside of their culture, they are usually placed in an awkward situation in which they are forced to leave their own culture and either embrace their spouse's culture or, even worse, be somewhere in between both realities. In some cases, Asian women are still able to maintain their cultural heritage but rarely are they able to bridge the cultural divide like Filipinas, where their spouses from a different culture are truly accepted or participate socially to such a degree as they do. Sadly, Asian women assume a somewhat submissive role in Asian society, and their ability to be the strong bridge between two worlds, as Filipinas are, never materializes. In addition, the history of colonization all over Asia has not produced the same results of openness and adaptability to other cultures as in the Philippines. Therefore, the Filipino people have benefitted in many ways from their maternal heritage, along with the historical events surrounding their people.

Having a strong maternal presence has been a positive attribute for the Filipino people. Filipinas who have spouses in the United States bridged the cultural gap between the two countries by being able to bring their Filipino family closer to the social realities found in this country, while their strength as maternal figures allowed them to also invite their non-Filipino spouses to encounter the Filipino culture in a positive manner. A similar dynamic can also be said to have occurred within the church. Just as the mothers are the maintainers of the home and church, Filipinas are also the ones able to create the necessary worship environment in the home and the church. The women are the ones who do the work to allow others to enter into the sacramental mysteries of the church. In the case of the Filipinas, they are also able to invite their own families into the sacred space of others because of the bridge formed through their interracial marriages. The sacred space invited into is not totally unfamiliar, since the nurturing presence is always there; new encounters, however, are ever present and can be openly embraced because of the maternal care and protection. In addition, those who were already established in the church become welcoming members in the resettlement process through a similar process of maternal care and compassion. Whether by coming together through faith as Catholics or in the home through marriage, Filipinas continue to allow others to bridge the cultural divide through their initial courage and triumph of navigating both worlds.

Conclusion

While the biological mixing of different peoples usually has a negative connotation associated with it for most Asians, the Filipino people have not taken their encounters with the foreign presence in the Philippines with the same attitude. Rather, the Filipino heart has embraced *mestizaje*—both cultural and biological mixing—as a positive attribute in their community. On the one hand, this Filipino way of thinking might be the byproduct of colonization, where the natives often felt a sense of inferiority in the midst of foreigners with their authoritative control over them. For example, similar to most European expansion at that time, the Spanish colonization of the Philippines brought along with it military might that included an atmosphere of pseudocultural and pseudo-spiritual superiority over indigenous practices found on the thousands of islands. Therefore, the mixing between the native islanders and the Spaniards was seen as a positive since Spanish blood made the people closer to becoming more like their "superior" colonizers. On the other hand, the embrace of *mestizaje* by the Filipino people can be viewed as a wonderful example of how humanity must embrace one another. Through linguistic, cultural, and biological mixtures, God's revelation is truly deepened not only by the Spirit revealed in such an embrace but also by the opportunity for something "new" to emerge from these encounters becoming possible.

It is not a secret that *mestizaje* is not an easy process for most—particularly not an Asian culture. The ability to see foreign influence in a positive light, even in an oppressive colonial situation, reveals the character of the Filipino people, one that involves both reconciliation and inculturation. Through the efforts of reconciliation and inculturation, involving not just forgiving the colonizers but also embracing the historical events from it as a positive development, the task of Christianity becomes evident in the Filipino people. This "newness" is the ongoing work of creation in which God created in the beginning, but the unfolding of his creation is ongoing. The task of Christians is to see Christ in one another, a task that requires us to see how the coming together, even biologically, of differing peoples allows a different perspective in regard to the incarnation.

Therefore, Filipino Catholics are both accustomed to and welcoming of the encounters with differing people. This characteristic goes beyond just "tasting" the richness of another culture to a true embrace revealed with their acceptance of biological mixture, an embrace that is usually very difficult for most Asians to accept. This ability to fully accept the other, then, makes the Filipino immigration experience much less a rupture with their past, including their homeland and heritage, and makes their embrace of a new home in another country a true reality. The Filipino American Catholic experience has been one that has been built on this foundation, one that is often gone unacknowledged or properly reflected on.

The Filipino community's resilience in the wake of their efforts at creating their own cultural worship space were thwarted due in large part to their homeland's previous experience of gathering as *communio*. Rather than falling into dejection, Filipino American Catholics were able to use the lessons of their faith journey back home, including their saint heroes, BCCs, etc., and once again transform their situation where the diversity of cultural backgrounds beyond just the Filipino people could once again be that *communio* with those already in existence here in the United States. This accommodation with other social and religious groups brought about a unity of faith just as back home when different island groups came together as a people of faith. The coming together, however, does not necessarily cause different groups to relinquish their distinct backgrounds but further reveals that true unity can only be achieved through diversity. Likewise, the coming together of Filipino American Catholics within the US Church did not erase the spirituality of the Filipino people, but through creative exercise, Filipino American Catholics were able once again to incorporate their cultural realities within the wider church. Therefore, celebrations previously mentioned continue to exist where there are Filipino Americans worshiping together and continue to include the next generation. One significant difference is that Filipino American Catholics have been able to maintain their cultural religious heritage while being immersed in the US Church, perhaps as a result of their cultural practice of hospitality. Other ethnic groups have been able to do the same but only in their separate communities.

Chapter 8

Toward the Need
for Theological Memory

The Korean American Catholic Experience

Korean immigrants in the first wave (1903–1945) were laborers seeking economic refuge, picture brides seeking social refuge, and activists seeking political refuge. The second wave, known as the postwar period, lasted from 1945–1965. Korean immigrants during this time period sought relief from the ravages of the Second World War and Korean War. From 1965 to the present, the third wave has been generically categorized as the post-1965 immigration period. Many Koreans during this period left for the U.S. out of economic concerns and make up the majority of the Korean American population. Today, a fourth wave is emerging as transnational mobility increases due to corporate and government activities within a global economy. Those in the latter wave are quite different than their predecessors as many come to the U.S. already educated, with vast resources, and the reality of one day returning back to Korea.[1]

Within the last wave in the post-1965 immigration era, developments both in the United States and in Korea have generated a complexity in describing the characteristics of immigrants during the last fifty years. Revisions to immigration legislation in the United States, especially in 1990 and in the aftermath of the IMF bailout of Korea later in that decade, when the financial crisis occurred, are just a few of the events that changed the immigration landscape for both the sending country and the receiving nation. Therefore, the post-1965 era of immigration should have two subdivisions with roughly the decade of the 1990s as a dividing line. Prior to this decade, the annual number of Korean immigrants gradually increased and peaked between 1976 and 1990.[2] In addition, the decrease of immigrants during the 1990s because of such factors previously mentioned did not last, as the adjustment during the decade led to slight increases in the new millennium and continues at a steady pace today. The pre-1990s Korean immigrants and their counterparts of the post-1990s are, however, quite different, since the reasons for departure from the homeland varied over time. Even though these two periods of immigration are divided by a decade, where the 1990s have significantly altered the characteristics of those immigrating to a new land, one characteristic remains constant in light of ongoing developments of Korea or the United States. The constant factor for immigration, regardless of economic and political stability, has been education. The educational opportunities found in the United States continue to be a prime motivating factor for leaving even the comforts of Korea. Both the "push" as well as the "pull" factors are in play here. The difficulty of receiving a good education in Korea because of unprecedented competitive levels continues to "push" Koreans to migrate elsewhere in hopes of better educational opportunities. The numerous opportunities for a good education found in the United States are the "pull" factors that continue to attract Korean immigrants. While the "push/pull" dynamics in other arenas of life have been similar in the past, today's Korean economic or political situation does not "push" as many abroad as in the past, nor do the advantages of a foreign country become enough of a "pull" factor. The education factor is, however, still a valid reason for Koreans willing to immigrate for better educational opportunities.

> The passage of the Immigration and Naturalization Act of 1965 has probably the most significant effect on the Korean American community. Although the immigration of Koreans to the United States is one century old, the Korean American community before

1965 was insignificant in terms of population size. . . . Thus the current Korean community in the United States is largely the by-product of the liberalization of immigration law in 1965.[3]

The fiftieth anniversary of the 1965 Hart-Celler Act, the act that changed the immigration landscape of the United States, provides us an occasion to see how various ethnic groups have developed in their new home country. While tracing their roots back to their homeland, the development of an immigrant people within the last fifty years has, in actuality, created a unique history for immigrants and their counterparts back home.

By preserving biological and linguistic characteristics along with certain cultural similarities, immigrants are still able to trace their roots to the history of their countries of origin and feel a sense of belonging with, and pride about, the developments back in the homeland. Different social and political developments back home and here in the United States, however, especially among the next generation, are creating the foundation for a different history to emerge, a natural result of the immigration process.

In the Korean American experience, many immigrants who came to the United States in the 1970s and 1980s continue to identify themselves as Koreans and call Korea their home country. This is not uncommon for the first generation, as their incorporation into the fabric of US society seems to be minimal due to the cultural and linguistic challenges continually confronting them. Their presence in the United States, however, has made them more of a permanent fixture in the United States than they themselves might assume. When recalling their history, Koreans of this immigrant generation will usually share the common events of Korea that led to their departure. In particular, the experiences of poverty before Korea emerged as a global leader, along with the lived trauma of the Korean War, usually stand out in their memory. The history after these two moments, however, is not always shared and has diverged in different ways. The experience of Korea emerging out of the ashes of war and poverty and achieving a position on the forefront of many industries today is not shared intimately by those living abroad, while the immigrant's own financial contributions back home are not always recognized in this successful growth. Although Korean Americans embrace the growth of Korea on the international stage with great pride, the developments leading to this outcome are not familiar to many living abroad. In other words, contemporary Korean society has moved beyond the common ground of poverty and war shared with immigrants; in essence, differing histories have emerged between those in Korea and those in diaspora.

Further exacerbating the historical distinctiveness between Koreans and Korean Americans is the fact that those who left the homeland do not fully represent the population back home. Rather, a distinct segment of the Korean population emigrated abroad. "They are a select group in terms of their demographic, socioeconomic, and religious characteristics."[4] Although the 1965 immigration legislation focused primarily on family reunification, occupational needs, and refugee asylum found in all sectors of society, Korean immigration has been quite unbalanced in that immigrants from this peninsular country have been primarily Christians. Pyong Gap Min states that the reasons why there has been an "overrepresentation of Christians among Korean immigrants" is that this immigrant group stems from three main demographics: an urban middle class population, Christians fleeing North Korea, and Westernized Korean Christians.[5]

Korean immigrants who left their homeland shortly after legislative reforms allowed them to do so departed without much expectation of returning one day. Many left under dire circumstances, and their connections back to their birthplace would be only in their memories or the longing for home in their hearts. Even with modern technologies and advances in aviation, international travel was still a luxury that would be experienced only once for many of the first who landed on US shores. The belief that they would be permanently leaving Korea behind and not returning was a common attitude embraced by the first half of the post-1965 wave of immigrants. Furthering this reality was the fact that many family members soon followed the initial immigrants and found their entire families relocating. The lack of familial ties to the Korean peninsula added to the reality that there was no returning to Korea. Only in the later half of the post-1965 immigration would the transnational movement be a reality.

Koreans use the saying that when a person thrives it is like a fish which finds its way to water. Likewise, a person who is not doing well is likened to a fish out of water. The waters the fish lives in are not questioned in one's homeland since the waters (e.g., environment, surrounding, etc.) are all the same. Immigrants realize, however, that not only are the waters different in various places but also that one must be especially conscious of the waters surrounding them. Thus, a sociologist living in the United States never imagined his journey for academic excellence would lead to "permanent" immigration. The career decisions, however, along with family life, have placed him in an unforeseen situation in which he now asks what kind of water he is willing to swim in, especially in light of his children's future.

This broadening experience of deepening the waters one swims in because of the immigration experience is an ongoing experience for future generations coming to the United States, a gift not only to the individual but also to the community as religious and social consciousness are heightened in differing environs. As with any encounter, this heightened awareness comes with either paralysis or growth. Either immigrants or their offspring find the deepening waters to be too difficult to navigate and never experience the depth and breadth of their environment as they continue a "ghetto-like" mentality, or they learn to swim in ever increasing challenges of life where new opportunities in the ways of self-expression and discovery fulfill immigrants and subsequent generations.

Scriptural Memory

> Rabbi Israel Ball Shem Tov once said,
> Forgetfulness leads to exile, while in remembrance lies the secret
> of redemption.[6]

In the Old Testament, the identification with the living God as passed on from Abraham to his offspring is a powerful reminder of the divine presence. Recalling the God of Abraham, of Isaac, and of Jacob gave the Israelites both a communal and religious identity whether they were in the Promised Land or in captivity elsewhere. The covenant between God and the chosen people was realized each and every time this historical reality was invoked. This sort of "mantra" on the motif of God, passed on from generation to generation, is significant in many ways. First, the figures associated with the divine name are remembered not only for being the first to encounter the living God but also as stalwart figures of the faith whose lives must be imitated, not because of their perfection in following God's calling in their lives, but rather as an example of how God's faithfulness in the covenant is realized throughout their lives, even in their own misgivings. Therefore, the patriarchs of Israel become an important way of remembering who God is and remembering God's merciful works performed through them on behalf of God's people.

Being reminded of God through the patriarchs begs the question of why the people needed such a method of remembrance when they were the chosen ones witnessing God's miraculous acts time and time again. One possible explanation for this repeated act was that this recitation was not just an act of remembrance in fear of forgetting but, rather, the act of reciting the lineage of their ancestors was also a method of resisting the temptation of the multitude of gods surrounding the Israelite people. The revelation of God to Abraham, Isaac, and Jacob was more than a disclosure of the Creator, as this engagement between the forefathers and the living God altered their whole way of life. By entering into this covenantal relationship and choosing to follow the God of their forefathers, the Israelites had to forsake all their former pagan ways. The surrounding land, however, was still filled with pagan rituals, and the multitude of gods remained a strong temptation for them even in the midst of their covenantal relationship. Therefore, the recital of who God is in relation to their ancestors became a technique used to resist the temptation of following false gods as well. The book of Judges recounts the many occasions in which the attraction of foreign culture and false gods of neighboring nations tempt God's people. The remembrance of the covenant is the remedy by which grace helps to both repel the surrounding temptations and help the Israelites stay faithful to the relationship with their true God.

Such recitations also serve as a form of storytelling. Without having to recount every specific detail of the story, those who are reminded of the God of Abraham, of Isaac, and of Jacob automatically hear what is needed in their lives, either the need for further fidelity or for gratitude for being invited into such a covenantal relationship. Contained in this mantra is not just one story but a plethora of stories of the Israelites' faith journey that also includes the formation of God's people. While the exodus event is the pivotal movement of God's salvation as expounded on in the last chapter, the remembering of God through one's ancestors must then begin with Abraham. The father of faith reminds God's people of their origin as migrants, especially since Abraham was called by God to go forth.

> The LORD said to Abram: Go forth from your land, your relatives, and from your father's house to a land that I will show you. I will make of you a great nation, and I will bless you; I will make your name great, so that you will be a blessing. I will bless those who bless you and curse those who curse you. All the families of the earth will find blessing in you. Abram went as the LORD directed him, and Lot went with him. Abram was seventy-five years old when he left Haran. Abram took his wife Sarai, his brother's son Lot, all the possessions that they had accumulated, and the persons they had acquired in Haran, and they set out for the land of Canaan. (Gen 12:1-5)

The lack of possessions, especially the protection of communal family, along with the insecurity of not possessing land, further reveals Abraham's vulnerability. Therefore, Abraham's own "exodus" from his people and birthplace is as much about the journey itself as it is about the new land to settle in. It is truly an invitation to witness the encounters of this life with that of the encounter with God.

Becoming a migrant—either voluntarily or involuntarily—is a central theme found within the Old and New Testament. In particular, the initial human encounter with the divine often involves a movement from the known to the unknown as characterized in the world of the migrant. In the Old Testament, the formation of God's people begins with Abram and Sarai's call to become Abraham and Sarah in a new land. The call to leave one's existing family, communal relationships and homeland made Abraham and Sarah migrants of their own choosing. Their choice to enter the world of migrants meant they would never fully settle in the lands they traveled in nor become part of the people and communities surrounding them. "In fact, it is Abraham's identity as [a nomadic foreigner] that directly facilitates the outworking of God's blessing given to Abraham in Genesis."[7]

The decision to leave their familiar environment represents a certain paradox for migrants such as Abraham and Sarah as they no longer rely on their own abilities, living as members of a society with certain rights, but instead join the ranks of those who are living on the margins of society. "In leaving Hārān, Abraham transferred the wellbeing and survival of his entire household to his new God."[8] In addition, Scripture is silent regarding Abraham's pedigree or why God would choose this individual over another. "It is thus that Abraham begins his entrance into literary fame as an unknown with no recorded personal achievements, no remarkable character traits, and no glorious past."[9] Thus, the lack of a notable reputation in his previous life contributes and even exacerbates the "nonexistence" of migrants on their journey and contributes to their vulnerability in a new land.

Being a migrant is not an identity that easily fades, especially if this new identity is part of God's plan for bestowing a universal blessing. Abraham and Sarah's willingness to live as migrants requires a lifetime and even their offspring continue a similar existence. The fact that no land was acquired during Abraham and Sarah's lifetime for their resettlement and only in Sarah's death is Abraham able to acquire a burial land, highlights the fact that no home is truly established. Abraham's description of himself as a *ger* (רֵג Gen 23:4) or resident alien stresses his migrant status.[10] In addition, his descendants carry on this legacy as nomadic foreigners even though they are born in a place entirely different than their parents and would never return to that homeland.

> Various biblical texts call Israel's ancestors *gerim* (גֵּרִים, the plural form of *ger*) or describe their activities in the land as those of immigrants. . . . Other biblical passages indicate that the people of Israel, the descendants of Abraham and Sarah, were also aliens or migrants, especially when they were slaves in Egypt and when they wandered in the wilderness.[11]

Abraham's status as a foreigner, a nomadic person, a migrant is further highlighted in his attempt to acquire a burial site for Sarah under the system of land rights then in place.[12] Abraham's status is revealed because he has no legal right to what the people hold most valuable and sacred—the land. "Abraham acknowledges that because of his low status as a resident sojourner he has no rights to land for burial."[13] The respect both parties involved have for one another, however, legitimizes the transaction and in the end, allows Abraham to acquire the burial site for his wife. The land acquired must be used in a specific manner because of an implicit understanding of what the land being transferred is intended for.[14] Thus, the newly acquired land is intended for Sarah's burial and all their future descendants. It is interesting to note that because this land is intended for the dead, the living still do not have any home to call their own.

It is most likely the stories of Abraham and Sarah were recounted during the Babylonian exile of the Israelites. Once again, God's people are without land, *eretz* (אֶרֶץ), while in captivity. Since their identity as God's people is tied to the Promised Land, the absence of one reflected the absence of the other. In order to reclaim their relationship with God, the Israelites had to either go back to the land provided them after their liberation from Egyptian captivity or rediscover their connection with God beyond just the land as their Babylonian captivity continued on. Therefore, the recitation of the God of Abraham, of Isaac, and of Jacob recalled their origins but also allowed the people to re-create their relationship with God. In the absence of the land of their heritage, those in captivity realize an emerging new identity through their encounters in a foreign *eretz*.

Human movement, by choice or by force, to a foreign *eretz*, entails more than the relocation or just the destination point. Rather, decisions for relocation—whether in biblical times or in today's reality—encompass a variety of reasons ranging from basic survival to other environmental factors. Could reasons such as these also have been Abraham's initial motivation for leaving his whole life (land, relations, and father's dwelling) behind? Abraham's departure from Ur transcends the confines of limitation and definitions of his former life and in his journey to a land unknown to him, he is able to gain self-awareness of his true origin—a life that originates from the divine and not his own. Since life arose from the earth through the divine breath, the *eretz* holds a special role in both the relationships of peoples to one another and with their God. Abraham's departure and journey represent the movement from a known *eretz* to an unknown *eretz*. In order for the promise of the blessing of a great nation to be realized, God's invitation must be accepted through such acts of faith.

This realization that Abraham and Sarah were afforded took their whole lifetime to materialize, further revealing God's patience with them. Although the goal of movements from one *eretz* to another *eretz* still remains the same, this is not often the reality of migrants today, since their struggle for daily existence obscures the freedom to follow God in previously unforeseen ways. Still, God is patient with us. The *eretz* promised by God to Abraham, then, is more than the physical land, but in the settling down in another locale, the value of self-discovery as well as a discovery of following God in an unprecedented manner becomes the true blessing to other nations as the divinity is more fully realized in our humanity.

Biblical narratives of migration, such as that of Abraham and Sarah embracing a new cultural religious identity through their migrant journey, are illustrated throughout the Scriptures. "Culture and ethnicity are central themes in scripture from Genesis to Revelation and play an integral part in God's plan for humanity."[15] Throughout salvation history, human movement from displacement to an encounter with the unknown leads to a new identity in God. This discovery also benefits those who walk with the migrant, as evident in those who entered into a relationship with Abraham and Sarah. Through an act of solidarity, the richness found in migration is shared with those welcoming the stranger into their midst. This pattern of the migrant church gives hope to generations to come. The Korean American Catholic experience engages many of these biblical themes, especially the call to "go forth." Blessings continue through a distinct people as well as to the land where they dwell through their development as a cultural-religious people.

Isaac also presents an interesting scenario within our faith narrative. His specific role in the *Akedah* story (the binding of Isaac) is applicable for many migrants today. Isaac is the one who demonstrates willingness to give up his life. The difficulties of this particular offering are revealed in struggles of a father and not the son whose life is at stake. Does Isaac's lack of resistance signify an innocence of trust in his father Abraham and in God, or does his silence show extreme ignorance or naïveté? Regardless, Isaac's preparedness to participate in God's request is not only about his father, nor just about himself, but also truly about the future generations to come. Along with the *Akedah* event, Isaac is associated with water wells as a builder of such systems where people gather to maintain their lives. Symbolically, the well of Isaac, coupled with the willingness to lay down his life for the fulfillment of God's promise of blessing to all nations, illustrates the pivotal act needed in migration for the well-being of future generations as the laying down of one's life in sacrifice is the foundation for future generations to build on.

Through Isaac's life, Jacob emerges as the next patriarch and is, at times, referred to as the "true" father of the Hebrew people since from his twelve sons emerge the twelve tribes of Israel. Those who subscribe to this notion that Jacob is the "real" father see the life of Abraham and the sparing of the life of Isaac as occurring for this purpose. Although the logic may be clear on this matter, questions still arise, since Jacob was not the rightful heir in the lineage. Rather, Jacob assumes this place out of trickery, since he deceived Isaac in his old age into giving him the blessing due his brother. Nevertheless, Jacob is remembered as part of the ancestors God has chosen to be remembered.

Rather than appealing to just the bloodline as the focal point of the Israelite's lineage from Abraham to Jacob, another rationale is needed for the practice of remembering God through one's ances-tors. Many parallels arise when the context of Abraham's journey is compared with that of his grandson, including the suspicious actions in certain situations. God, however, is more concerned about the willingness to migrate than these moments of deception and distrust, as illustrated by these two patriarchs. The events surrounding the famine during the time of Jacob and his twelve sons eventually lead them to Egypt, another movement from a known *eretz* to an unknown *eretz*, paralleling his grandparent's journey from their homeland. Thus, by following a similar motif of his forefather, but under differing conditions, Jacob's journey resembles that of Abraham's own calling forth and continues God's blessing to all.

The remembrance of who God is as the God of Abraham, of Isaac, and of Jacob was a selective way of remembering events that were vital to the identity and faith journey of the people of Israel—whether in the homeland or away in captivity. Since our reality is not captured as a complete recording of every detail but rather in fragments that are cherished but which also traumatize, these memories are either retained and serve a purpose for our identity or otherwise vanish from our memory. Memories are stories of the pieces of our lives that mean something to us, as well as events that need to be told and remembered for future generations. Again, these are fragmented realities that include negative aspects as il-lustrated by the misgivings of the patriarchs. Yet the combination of all that is remembered presents a fabric of not only who God is but also what is important in this encounter—the journeying from a known *eretz* to an unknown *eretz*. Therefore, the recalling of the divine by the Israelites in this manner provides the modus to retain their faith and identity within a specific genre.

Conclusion

Although Koreans and Korean immigrants are two distinct people with differing historical markers, especially as the com-mon grounds become more of a distant memory, other factors also exists in this divide. An often overlooked way of maintaining some common ground that could be used in linking the two groups is the financial support by immigrant groups to their counterparts back home. Often unacknowledged is the way Korean Americans have contributed to the growth of Korea, especially through financial means. In the early decades (1970s and 1980s) of Korean immigration, those living in the United States supported the building of the Korean infrastructure. In particular, the financial contributions sent back to the homeland have never been properly documented and recognized. Without such support, the building of churches and education of the clergy would have taken longer for the Korean Church.

Today, many Korean American Catholic communities are ministered to by visiting Korean priests who view these faith communities as an extension of clergy's own diocese in Korea. Thus, collections for ongoing ministry, as well as capital campaigns for buildings, are still being requested from those living in the United States. Korean Americans still support in some fashion the church in Korea as well as her missionary activities in Latin America and Africa. Contributions such as these are vital as key historical markers and connections allowing those living in this country to share in the social and ecclesial successes back home. Many of the sacrifices such as these, however, go unaccounted for, thus exacerbating the differences in historical development. Therefore, the history of Koreans and Korean Americans is diverging further and further on different courses.

More and more, even if proper acknowledgment were given to Korean Americans, they find themselves as a distinct people because of their own encounters in the United States. Without the recent connections to the developments in Korea, immigrants lack the stories that help define them and give reason for their existence. Beyond the common stories of poverty and war in Korea prior to immigration, Korean Americans lack stories—historical or a metanarrative—that would identify them as a distinct group with an origin and purpose for being in the United States.

Rupture, then, is not simply the fact of being taken away from a place willingly or unwillingly. Rather, rupture is the removal from one's locale while at the same time losing the narratives that shape an entire people. The poverty and war many immigrants experienced when they departed in the 1970s and 1980s were never continued or linked with the stories of resettlement for their off-spring. Leaving desperate situations behind to enter a foreign land must have had its own challenges that were endurable because of the hope afforded by the American dream. These challenges were not, however, collected, shared, or—worse yet—sacralized by the immigrant community as a way of continuing on a heritage, in-dividual traditions, or a narrative connecting those in the United States with the homeland. Instead, Korean immigrants identified with events in Korea and failed to establish a historical continuity for the next generation. The gap in historical narrative is a rupture that needs rediscovery and healing of memories for future genera-tions and immigrants still to come.

The lack of a historical memory for Korean immigrants in the United States becomes problematic since the linkage to the home-land has to go back to the 1960s and 1970s, while their counterparts have matured from those events. Although contemporary Korean accomplishments in the social, political, and cultural arenas can be equally shared with those living in diaspora, they do not truly represent the people abroad in their new context. The events back home begin a new formulation of a people in terms of mind-set, appearance, mannerisms, etc., while those abroad are relegated to a passive role as spectators. Koreans today are different from their counterparts who initially immigrated after the 1965 immigration reforms mainly due to the democratic reforms of the 1980s, the economic developments which lifted the country out of poverty (even to levels beyond those living in diaspora), and the global attraction to Korean culture through Korean TV dramas and music sensations. Such developments in the homeland can be embraced with much pride by those in diaspora; the cultural, social, and political transformation that define a people, however, cannot be equally shared by those on the outside. The difference between the two is that those on the inside either knowingly or unknow-ingly actively participate in the developments of the country while those on the outside passively observe these events. The former transforms the people as a group into "something other," while the latter retains characteristics similar to when they immigrated as well as transforming them into "something other" while in their new homeland.

This "something other" is not only hard to define but also very difficult to embrace—even by the immigrant generation. For instance, this "something other" is labeled as being Korean American for those living in the United States who are of Korean descent. The first generation, however, identify themselves completely as Korean and not Korean American. Likewise, subsequent generations may identify with being American and have nothing to do with their Korean heritage. Each instance reveals the inability to embrace the development of the "something other." Becoming "something other" is, however, a reality for those who departed the homeland and those still in Korea. Often we label the "something other" as a generational or cultural difference when in fact we are always developing, adapting, and transforming into new realities based on the historical narratives that help identify who we are. These foundations are taken for granted in the homeland for they exist "naturally" there. They are, however, harder to uncover and identify in diaspora since the embrace of becoming "something other" does not happen as naturally as back in the homeland, and such recognition requires tools and skills that the initial generation might not possess.

Abraham, Isaac and Jacob were all able to embrace this "something other" as their own identity in the faith journey. They are still remembered today for their ability to do so, a powerful reminder for everyone affected by a world church in our backyard. The purpose of reciting the mantra—the God of Abraham, of Isaac, and of Jacob—acts both as a method of remembrance and a way of resisting temptation. Today's calling on the divine in the same manner continues this heritage of overcoming the temptations of following false avenues to the way of authenticity by reminding us that the encounter of this "something other" becomes our true testament as God's people in a world church in our backyard.

Conclusion

Unity through Diversity

From her very beginnings, diversity has been one of the key elements of the local and universal church. St. Paul reminds us of this when he mentions the variety of gifts that the members of the one body possess (1 Cor 12:12-14). The dynamics of this diversity are not merely functional but also refer to cultural and ethnic differences of God's people that enriched the early communities, since these characteristics encompass the whole person. In short, the complete person is the gift which fulfills the Body of Christ. Again, this diversity involving the entire person is seen in the Acts of the Apostles where the descent of the Holy Spirit at Pentecost brought many peoples from various parts of the then-known world together as believers in the one Lord. This account in Acts 2:2-12 tells us that the multitude underwent a conversion to praise the risen Christ in a multitude of languages. From the very beginnings of the church, local faith communities embraced and grew from the diversity of cultures and peoples. Thus, the prophetic beginnings of the nascent church foreshadowed the diversity of the universal church contained within her members.

> It is the "tradition" of the church, in the transmission of this life with all its diverse expressions, that diversities which might have proved discordant were harmonized. The danger then is of a certain levelling out, as it were the emasculation of differences which are also riches, riches by which the church lives.[1]

The stress on unity has often come at the cost of diversity throughout church history. While the encounter with diverse peoples and cultures came naturally with the spread of the Good News, the compromise reached at the Council of Jerusalem was not as easily replicated with every new encounter. Therefore, the stress on unity rather than diversity was always a strong temptation, especially when the sheer numbers of diverse peoples overwhelmed the encounter. The lone focus on unity often led to uniformity, one way of incorporating those coming into the church from diverse backgrounds. Uniformity, then, was the insurance policy when diversity disrupted the life of the church. Yves Congar uses the dating of Easter to illustrate the diversity in the church and how uniformity won out even when unity was not at stake.[2] Christians did not question the central doctrine of their belief—the death and resurrection of Christ. The dating of this important feast day, however, came under question depending on which calendar was being used. Rather than allowing diverse cultural expressions of Easter within differing locales, uniformity of this liturgical celebration was desired by both civil and ecclesiastical leaders in control.

> Unity called for uniformity. Rome, the centre of the empire and of Catholicity, was designated to ensure this uniformity of observance. Rome took the charge very much to heart and saw it as an expression of concern for the unity of the church. . . . Constantine was concerned to establish a unity which was at the same time both that of the church and that of the empire.[3]

While uniformity relies on a hierarchical power willing to enforce it from the top down, unity allowing for diversity does not appeal to similar rationales for its existence. After all, the appeal to apostolic succession did not allow for such differences to coexist when there were no doctrinal issues involved.

Romanticizing the apostolic church leads to envisioning that period of church life as an undivided church living in a unity of faith that was somehow later disrupted by diversity in cultures, peoples, and theological reflections. Thus, one of the main motivations for wanting a uniform church is our own attempts at returning to an "ecclesial state of perfection"; such an existence, however, was never a reality for the early church. While as followers of Christ, a unity of faith is always a primary concern, differences in expressing such truths have always been with the church from her inception.[4]

Today's world church presents similar challenges faced by the church throughout history. The question still remains, how does a community of faith ensure the unity of faith while allowing for such diversity? Rather than longing for a unified church that never existed by enacting regulations and practices of uniformity, we would be better served to expend such energies in embracing differences that transform all peoples and cultures involved. The acknowledgment that diversity existed from the very beginning of the church's existence is the first step in embracing a world church in our backyard, since this guides our intentions in allowing faith communities to create both ethnic churches as well as multicultural ones as directed by the diversity in our midst.

An Ongoing Pentecost: An Ecclesial Gift

In every generation, the Holy Spirit continues the work of Pentecost. In particular, the work of the Spirit allows glimpses of the prophetic beginnings where diversity of peoples and cultures from the ends of the earth came together to enrich the early church. The Spirit also provides insights into how today's diversity is a sign of the unique beginnings of our faith as well as the ongoing work of the church in embracing all peoples with differing backgrounds. Therefore, the work of Asian and Pacific Island faith communities in the US Catholic Church is not just a natural progression of all ethnic communities once they reach certain stages of maturity. Rather, the contributions of Asian and Pacific Island Catholics are a reflection of the initial diversity of the nascent church, and more importantly, a deeper revelation of the ecclesial reality—a striving for unity through diversity. Therefore, the Asian and Pacific Island Catholic presence is an unveiling of the diverse attributes of God found within the *Imago Dei* of each of our brothers and sisters.

Today, Asian and Pacific Island Catholics are deeply indebted to the work of Hispanic/Latino and African American Catholics in the United States. Their presence and activity have benefitted all minority faith communities. Their leadership and achievements are examples and hopes for all faith communities. Through their commitment and sacrifice to both church and society, other ethnic groups such as Asian and Pacific Island Catholics are being recognized at every social and ecclesial level and encouraged to mature in a similar manner. Thus, we are truly grateful for the Hispanic/ Latino and African American presence as they, too, represent the diversity of the early church and the deeper calling to embrace the differences of culture and people surrounding us today.

Asian and Pacific Island Catholics are following a similar trajectory in maturation in the US Catholic Church. Following previous examples, Catholics of Asian and Pacific Island descent are realizing their place in US society and beginning to carve out their home in the church. Within each minority group, a greater consciousness of being part of the US church along with their ecclesial contribution is beginning to emerge—the ongoing gift of the Spirit in allowing this generation to see the diverse beginnings of the past and the future direction of the church in embracing diversity in all areas of life. This contribution is not a repetitive movement of the past but, rather, the unfolding of God's calling to be a church engaged in the world. Therefore, the presence of Asian and Pacific Island Catholics in the US Catholic Church today is a recognition and furthering of the previous work of Hispanic/Latinos and African American Catholics—a deeper reality based the work of those who have gone before us while engaging the current challenges of gathering and developing as local faith communities within the wider context of a global church.

The main challenge of Asian and Pacific Island Catholics coming together as a people of God is the diversity within this subcategory of the US Catholic population, a subgroup not developed within but rather lumped together by social, political and ecclesial conditions. This forced composition initially presents the difficult challenges of gathering peoples without common histories, languages or cultures. Others who have gone before Asian and Pacific Island Catholics did not have to overcome this additional hurdle as most ethnic communities enjoyed a common social and/or ecclesial history as well as a unifying language and culture. For example, African American Catholics rallied around their common history of oppression in the United States and garnered national support in overcoming their struggles. Although Hispanic/Latinos Catholics possess a more diverse history depending on their country of origin, they are still united in the common history of European conquest and the origins of their Spanish-speaking cultural expressions.

In contrast, Asian and Pacific Island Catholics share none of these characteristics in enough length or depth to "naturally" bind the people of this subgroup. Through convenience, or rather misunderstanding, Asian and Pacific Island Catholics have come under one umbrella in the US Catholic Church and society. Thus, the challenges of embracing the diversity of language, people and cultures from Asia and the Pacific Islands are truly the unfolding of God's prophetic call for us to be a universal church through the diversity of her members gathered from all the ends of the earth. Asian and Pacific Island Catholics continue to reveal the multi-faceted dimensions of the divine through the presence of God's people and the challenge of the church to not only embrace this diversity but also to incorporate it within her membership to truly be the Body of Christ, the Word made flesh. Today, these differences allow the church to continue its mission initiated at Pentecost, thereby revealing to both within and outside her members her ecclesial reality.

Through the guidance of the Holy Spirit, Asian and Pacific Island Catholics are currently realizing their presence and contribution to their own as well as the universal church. Therefore, they are unifying to complete the ecclesial task entrusted to them. By coming together as one group, regardless of the challenges previously unforeseen, the prophetic nature of this necessary work emerges. By collaborating on a national pastoral plan, Asian and Pacific Island Catholics make their presence known in the wider church by demonstrating the deeper realities of what it means to be part of the one, holy, catholic, and apostolic church in this day and age. Furthermore, an episcopal response to the wider church based on the Asian and Pacific Island social, political, and ecclesial experience lived out with its unique expressions in the United States is a prophetic unveiling on how to be a church for generations to come. The overcoming of differences united within a social, political, and ecclesial structure reveals how the Spirit is able to overcome human barriers and fulfill the ecclesial mission of spreading the Good News. By modeling church as *communio*, Asian and Pacific Island Catholics hope to share a renewed vision of the Pentecost and a church relevant for us today and future generations of believers.

Notes

Introduction

1. Bible translations are taken from the *New American Bible*.

2. Thorsten Prill, "Migration, Mission and the Multi-Ethnic Church," *Evangelical Review of Theology* 33, no. 4 (2009): 333.

3. Ibid., 334.

4. Ibid., 342.

5. Ibid., 342–343; Cf. Ajith Fernando, *Acts*, The NIV Application Commentary (Grand Rapids, MI: Zondervan, 1998), 419.

6. Silvano Tomasi, "Migration and Catholicism in a Global Context," *Concilium* 5 (2008): 15.

Chapter 1

1. Richard Gaillardetz, "The Church as Sacrament: Towards an Ecclesial Spirituality," *The Way: Supplement* (1999): 23.

2. Patrick Granfield, "The Church as *Societas Perfecta* in the Schemata of Vatican I," *Church History* 48 (1979): 431–32.

3. Ibid., 440.

4. Gaillardetz, "Church as Sacrament," 23.

5. Second Vatican Council, *Sacrosanctum Concilium* (Constitution on the Sacred Liturgy), in *Vatican Council II: Constitutions, Decrees, Declarations; The Basic Sixteen Documents*, ed. Austin Flannery (Collegeville, MN: Liturgical Press, 2014). All quotations from the Vatican II documents are taken from this translation.

6. For an overview of historical development of liturgical translation, see Ian Paton, "*Sacrosanctum Concilium*: Fifty Years On," The Expository Times 125, no. 4 (2013): 158–62.

7. Ibid., 163.

8. Ibid., 165; Cf. SC 37–40.

9. Claire Johnson, et al., "*Sacrosanctum Concilium* at Fifty: Reports from Five English-Speaking Countries," *Worship* 87, no. 6 (2013): 482–516.

10. Paul Inwood, "England and Wales," in "*Sacrosanctum Concilium* at Fifty: Reports from Five English-Speaking Countries," *Worship* 87, no. 6 (2013): 502.

11. Ibid., 503.

12. Since many Korean American Catholic communities are staffed by clergy on temporary assignment from Korea, the Catholic Bishops' Conference of Korea (CBCK) and the United States Catholic Conference of Bishops (USCCB) work together in promoting the faith of those of Korean descent residing in the United States.

Chapter 2

1. Norman Tanner, *The Church and the World: Gaudium et Spes, Inter Mirifica* (Mahwah, NJ: Paulist Press, 2005), 14.

2. Ibid.

3. Ibid., 17–18.

4. Marie-Dominique Chenu, "Les signes des temps: réflexion théologique," in *L'Église Dans Le Monde De Ce Temps. Constitution pastorale "Gaudium et spes" (Unam Sanctam, 65b)* ed. Yves Congar and M. Peuchmard (Paris: Les Éditions Du Cerf, 1967), 225. See also Chenu, "Les signes des temps," 29–30, http://www.nrt.be/docs/articles/1965/87-1/1508-Les+signes+des+temps.pdf.

5. Joseph Komonchak, "The 'Legislative History' of *Gaudium et Spes*: An Original Tension Among Views at Vatican II and Interpretations of Catholic Social Thought," *Journal of Law, Philosophy and Culture* 2, no. 1 (2008): 94, 95, and 114.

6. Denis Edwards, *Breath of Life: A Theology of the Creator Spirit* (Maryknoll, NY: Orbis Books, 2004), 1.

7. Ibid., 38–39, 43.

8. Joseph Komonchak, "U.S. Bishops' Suggestions for Vatican II," https://jakomonchak.files.wordpress.com/2012/01/us-bishops-suggestions-for-vatican-ii.pdf, 28–29.

9. Ibid., 30.

10. Ibid., 30 and 44.

11. Tanner, *The Church and the World*, 23.

12. Russell Shaw, *American Church: The Remarkable Rise, Meteoric Fall, and Uncertain Future of Catholicism in America* (San Francisco: Ignatius Press, 2013), 183.

Chapter 3

1. Melissa J. Wilde, *Vatican II: A Sociological Analysis of Religious Change* (Princeton, NJ: Princeton University Press, 2007), 38.

2. Ibid., 41.

3. Ibid., 58–59.

4. Personal interview conducted on June 11, 2014.

5. Sentiments expressed by Bishop McNaughton on June 11, 2014.

6. Woll Ki Chung, "Small Christian Community and Communion Ecclesiology of Vatican II in the Catholic Church in Korea" [in Korean], in *"New Evangelization" and the Catholic Church in Korea: In Commemoration of the 50th Anniversary of Vatican Council II* (Seoul: Sogang University, 2012), 108.

7. Seil Oh, "Korean Catholic Church's Social Engagement after Vatican II: Religiosity and Spirituality" [in Korean], in *"New Evangelization" and the Catholic Church in Korea*, 130.

8. Ibid.

9. Hae Young Choi, "Change of Religious Life and Women's Identity after Vatican Council II" [in Korean], in *"New Evangelization" and the Catholic Church in Korea*, 143.

10. In-Cheol Kang, "The Korean Catholic Church's Social Participation and the Second Vatican Council" [in Korean], *Research Journal of Korean Church History* 25 (2005): 22.

11. Ibid., 23.

12. Ibid.

13. Ibid., 37.

14. Ibid., 40.

15. Ibid., 42.

Chapter 4

1. Hyun Sook Kim and Pyong Gap Min, "The Post-1965 Korean Immigrants: Their Characteristics and Settlement Patterns," *Korea Journal of Population and Development* 21, no. 2 (1992): 121.

2. Ibid., 122.

3. Lyndon B. Johnson, "Remarks at the Signing of the Immigration Bill, Liberty Island, New York, October 3, 1965," http://www.lbjlib.utexas.edu/johnson/archives.hom/speeches.hom/651003.asp.

4. Ibid.

5. Ibid.

6. Ibid.

7. Ibid.

8. Ibid.

9. Martin Luther King Jr., *Why We Can't Wait*, King Legacy (Boston: Beacon Press, 2010), 18–19.

10. Ibid., 44–45, 52.

11. Ibid., 20.

12. Ross Douthat, *Bad Religion: How We Became a Nation of Heretics* (New York: Free Press, 2012), 45–46.

Chapter 6

1. Min Zhou and Carl Bankston, *Straddling Two Social Worlds: The Experience of Vietnamese Refugee Children in the United States*, Urban Diversity Series no. 111 (New York: Institute for Urban and Minority Education, 2000), 5.

2. Ibid., 9.

3. Ibid., 9–10.

4. Don Thu Nguyen, "Reminiscences," in *Boat People: Personal Stories from the Vietnamese Exodus; 1975–1996*, ed. Carina Hoang (New York: Beaufort Books, 2013), 38.

5. Loc Mai, "Live to Tell Our Tale," in Hoang, *Boat People*, 14.

6. Thien Nga Le and Lilly Ngo, "Life Is Beautiful," in Hoang, *Boat People*, 219.

7. Mai, "Live to Tell our Tale," 14.

8. Zhou and Bankston, *Straddling Two Social Worlds*, 15.

9. Mai Phuong, *Stories of a Time* (Costa Mesa, CA: Vietbooks, 2011), 205–6.

10. Mai Phuong, *Autumn* (Costa Mesa, CA: Vietbooks, 2005), 233.

11. Nga Le and Ngo, "Life Is Beautiful," 220.

12. Minh Hoang Phan, "Which Path Should I Choose," in Hoang, *Boat People*, 165.

13. Anthony Nguyen, "SOS: You and God Save Us," in Hoang, *Boat People*, 95.

14. Interview with Vincent Pham on August 31, 2015.

15. Zhou and Bankston, *Straddling Two Social Worlds*, 21.

16. Peter Phan, *Vietnamese-American Catholics* (Mahwah, NJ: Paulist Press 2005), 69.

17. Linh Hoang, "Vietnamese Catholics and Diaspora: Re-imaging Mary as Vietnamese," World Catholicism Week, DePaul University, 2014.

18. Ibid.

19. Ibid.

20. Julio X. Labayen, "Vatican II in Asia and the Philippines," *The Ecumenical Review* 37, no. 3 (1985): 275.

21. Phan, *Vietnamese-American Catholics*, 101–3.

22. Ibid., 103.

Chapter 7

1. Migration Policy Institute, "RAD Diaspora File: The Filipino Diaspora in the United States," (July 2014): 4, http://www.migrationpolicy.org/research/select-diaspora-populations-united-states.

2. Maurizio Ambrosini, "Protected but Separated: International Immigrants in the Italian Catholic Church," in *Migration, Transnationalism, and Catholicism: Global Perspectives* (Basingstoke, UK: Palgrave Macmillan, 2016), forthcoming.

3. Virgil Mayor Apostol, *Way of the Ancient Healer: Sacred Teachings from the Philippine Ancestral Traditions* (Berkeley, CA: North Atlantic Books, 2010), 58.

4. Ibid., 53.

5. Julio X. Labayen, "Vatican II in Asia and the Philippines," *The Ecumenical Review* 37, no. 3 (1985): 275–82, 276.

6. Ibid., 275.

7. Ibid., 277.

Chapter 8

1. Simon C. Kim, *Memory and Honor: Cultural and Generational Ministries with Korean American Communities* (Collegeville, MN: Liturgical Press, 2013), 44.

2. Pyong Gap Min, "The Immigration of Koreans to the United States: A Review of Forty-Five Year (1965–2009) Trends," in *Koreans in North America: Their Twenty-First Century Experiences*, ed. Pyong Gap Min (Lanham, MD: Lexington Books, 2013), 12.

3. Hyun Sook Kim and Pyong Gap Min, "The Post-1965 Korean Immigrants: Their Characteristics and Settlement Patterns," *Korea Journal of Population and Development* 21, no. 2 (1992): 122.

4. Ibid., 128.

5. Ibid., 136–37.

6. Lesli Koppelman Ross, "The Importance of Remembering: The Best Way to Honor the Memory of Holocaust Victims Is Through Jewish Continuity," My Jewish Learning, http://www.myjewishlearning.com/article/the-importance-of-remembering/. The source of this quote from Rabbi Tov is unknown.

7. Sarita Gallagher, "Abraham on the Move: The Outpouring of God's Blessing through a Migrant," in *God's People on the Move: Biblical and Global Perspectives on Migration and Mission*, ed. vanThahn Nguyen and John Prior (Eugene, OR: Wipf and Stock, 2014), 4.

8. Ibid., 7.

9. Ibid., 6.

10. Timothy Lenchak, "Israel's Ancestors as Gerim: A Lesson of Biblical Hospitality," in Nguyen and Prior, *God's People on the Move*, 20.

11. Ibid.

12. Stephen Russell utilizes the system of land rights from anthropologist Max Gluckman in Stephen C. Russell, "Abraham's Purchase of Ephron's Land," *Biblical Interpretation* 21, no. 2 (2013): 153–70.

13. Ibid., 170.

14. Ibid., 162.

15. Fred Gringrich and Bradford Smith, "Culture and Ethnicity in Christianity/Psychology Integration: Review and Future Directions," *Journal of Psychology and Christianity* 33, no. 2 (2014): 140.

Conclusion

1. Yves Congar, *Diversity and Communion* (Mystic, CT: Twenty-Third Publications, 1985), 14.

2. Ibid., 16.

3. Ibid.

4. Ibid., 168.

Bibliography

Ambrosini, Maurizio. "Protected but Separated: International Immigrants in the Italian Catholic Church." In *Migration, Transnationalism, and Catholicism: Global Perspectives*. Basingstoke, UK: Palgrave Macmillan. Forthcoming.

Andres, Tomas, and Pilar Corzaon Nada-Andres. *Understanding the Filipino*. Quezon City, Philippines: New Day Publishers, 1987.

Apostol, Virgil Mayor. *Way of the Ancient Healer: Sacred Teachings from the Philippine Ancestral Traditions*. Berkeley, CA: North Atlantic Books, 2010.

Center for Immigration Studies. "Three Decades of Mass Immigration: The Legacy of the 1965 Immigration Act." 1995. http://www.cis.org/1965/ImmigrationAct-MassImmigration.

Chenu, Marie-Dominique. "Les signes des temps: réflexion théologique." In *L'Église dans le monde de ce temps. Constitution pastorale "Gaudium et Spes" (Unam Sanctam, 65b)*, edited by Yves Congar and M. Peuchmard, 205–25. Paris: Les Éditions Du Cerf, 1967.

———. "Les signes des temps." 29–39. http://www.nrt.be/ docs/articles /1965/87-1/1508-Les+signes+des+temps.pdf.

Congar, Yves. *Diversity and Communion*. Mystic, CT: Twenty-Third Publications, 1985.

De Guia, Katrin. *Kapwa: The Self in the Other; Worldviews and Lifestyles of Filipino Culture-Bearers*. Pasig City, Philippines: Anvil Publishing, 2005.

Douthat, Ross. *Bad Religion: How We Became a Nation of Heretics*. New York: Free Press, 2012.

Edwards, Denis. *Breath of Life: A Theology of the Creator Spirit*. Maryknoll, NY: Orbis Books, 2004.

Faggioli, Massimo. *Vatican II: The Battle for Meaning*. Mahwah, NJ: Paulist Press, 2012.

———. "Vatican II and the Church of the Margins." *Theological Studies* 74 (2013): 808–18.

Gaillardetz, Richard. "The Church as Sacrament: Towards an Ecclesial Spirituality." *The Way: Supplement* (1999): 22–34.

Gallagher, Sarita. "Abraham on the Move: The Outpouring of God's Blessing through a Migrant." In *God's People on the Move: Biblical and Global Perspectives on Migration and Mission*, edited by vanThahn Nguyen & John Prior, 3–17. Eugene, OR: Wipf and Stock, 2014.

Granfield, Patrick. "The Church as *Societas Perfecta* in the Schemata of Vatican I." *Church History* 48 (1979): 431–46.

Gringrich, Fred, and Bradford Smith. "Culture and Ethnicity in Christianity/Psychology Integration: Review and Future Directions." *Journal of Psychology and Christianity* 33, no. 2 (2014): 139–55.

Hoang, Carina, ed. *Boat People: Personal Stories from the Vietnamese Exodus 1975–1996*. New York: Beaufort Books, 2013.

Johnson, Clare, Bill Burke, Paul Inwood, Patrick Jones, and Paul Turner. "*Sacrosanctum Concilium* at Fifty: Reports from Five English-Speaking Countries." *Worship* 87, no. 6 (2013): 482–516.

Johnson, Lyndon B. "Remarks at the Signing of the Immigration Bill, Liberty Island, New York October 3, 1965. http://www.lbjlib.utexas.edu/johnson/ archives.hom/speeches.hom/651003.asp.

Kim, Simon C. *Memory and Honor: Cultural and Generational Ministries with Korean American Communities*. Collegeville, MN: Liturgical Press, 2013.

Kim, Sook Hyun, and Pyong Gap Min. "The Post-1965 Korean Immigrants: Their Characteristics and Settlement Patterns." *Korea Journal of Population and Development* 21, no. 2 (1992): 121–43.

King, Jr., Martin Luther. *A Testament of Hope: The Essential Writings and Speeches of Martin Luther King, Jr.* Edited by James Washington. New York: HarperCollins, 1991.

———. *Why We Can't Wait*. Boston: Beacon Press, 2011.

Komonchak, Joseph. "The 'Legislative History' of *Gaudium et Spes*: An Original Tension among Views at Vatican II and Interpretations of Catholic Social Thought." *Journal of Law, Philosophy and Culture* 2, no. 1 (2008): 89–120.

———. "U.S. Bishops' Suggestions for Vatican II." 1–45. https://jakomonchak.files.wordpress.com/2012/01/us-bishops-suggestions-for-vatican-ii.pdf.

Labayen, Julio X. "Vatican II in Asia and the Philippines." *The Ecumenical Review* 37, no. 3 (1985): 275–82.

Lenchak, Timothy. "Israel's Ancestors as Gerim: A Lesson of Biblical Hospitality." In *God's People on the Move: Biblical and Global Perspectives on Migration and Mission*, edited by vanThahn Nguyen and John Prior, 18–28. Eugene, OR: Wipf and Stock, 2014.

McNamara, Keith, and Jeanne Batalova. "The Filipino Diaspora in the United States." Migration Policy Institute (2015). http://www.migration policy.org/article/ filipino-immigrants-united-states.

Migration Policy Institute. "RAD Diaspora File: The Filipino Diaspora in the United States." (July 2014): 1–13. http://www.migrationpolicy .org/research/select-diaspora-populations-united-states.

Min, Pyong Gap. "The Immigration of Koreans to the United States: A Review of Forty-Five Year (1965–2009) Trends." In *Koreans in North America: Their Twenty-First Century Experiences*, edited by Pyong Gap Min, 9–34. Lanham, MD: Lexington Books, 2013.

Nguyen, Gia Kieng. *Whence . . . Wither . . . Vietnam?: A New Assessment of Vietnam's Predicament*. Translated by Ngoc Phach Nguyen. Paris: Canh Nam, 2005.

Phan, Peter. *Vietnamese-American Catholics*. Mahwah, NJ: Paulist Press, 2005.

Phuong, Mai. *Autumn*. Costa Mesa, CA: Vietbooks, 2005.

———. *Stories of a Time*. Costa Mesa, CA: Vietbooks, 2011.

Prill, Thorsten. "Migration, Mission and the Multi-Ethnic Church." *Evangelical Review of Theology* 33, no. 4 (2009): 332–46.

Russell, Stephen C. "Abraham's Purchase of Ephron's Land." *Biblical Interpretation* 21, no. 2 (2013): 153–70.

Shaw, Russell. *American Church: The Remarkable Rise, Meteoric Fall, and Uncertain Future of Catholicism in America*. San Francisco: Ignatius Press, 2013.

Stoney, Sierra, and Jeanne Batalova. "Filipino Immigrants in the United States." *Migration Information Source*. www.migrationpolicy.org/ article/filipino-immigrants-united-states.

Tanner, Norman. *The Church and the World:* Gaudium et Spes, Inter Mirifica. Mahwah, NJ: Paulist Press, 2005.

Tomasi, Silvano. "Migration and Catholicism in a Global Context." *Concilium* 5 (2008): 13–31.

USCCB. *Harmony in Faith: Korean American Catholics*. Washington, DC: USCCB Communications, 2015.

———. *Resettling in Place: Vietnamese American Catholics*. Washington, DC: USCCB Communications, 2015.

Zhou, Min, and Carl Bankston. *Straddling Two Social Worlds: The Experience of Vietnamese Refugee Children in the United States*. Urban Diversity Series No. 111. New York: Institute for Urban and Minority Education, 2000.

Index